Love Line

Love Line

GRISH DAVTIAN

RESOURCE *Publications* • Eugene, Oregon

LOVE LINE

Copyright © 2022 Grish Davtian. All rights reserved. Except for brief quotations in critical publications or reviews, no part of this book may be reproduced in any manner without prior written permission from the publisher. Write: Permissions, Wipf and Stock Publishers, 199 W. 8th Ave., Suite 3, Eugene, OR 97401.

Resource Publications
An Imprint of Wipf and Stock Publishers
199 W. 8th Ave., Suite 3
Eugene, OR 97401

www.wipfandstock.com

PAPERBACK ISBN: 978-1-6667-5499-5
HARDCOVER ISBN: 978-1-6667-5500-8
EBOOK ISBN: 978-1-6667-5501-5

AUGUST 17, 2022 11:05 AM

Contents

*** | 1

MOST DESIRED | 2

BETRAYAL | 4

THE OLD SONG OF GUITAR | 5

REMINDER | 6

HOT WITH LOVE | 7

PRAYER | 8

SPRING NIGHT | 9

DAYS ON | 11

QUEST | 13

OF FEELING, OF LOVE, OF DEVOTION, OF LONGING AND OF MEMORY | 14

ONCE UPON A TIME | 15

OF WINTER | 17

BLAZE OF LOVE | 18

INFINITY | 19

SPRING IS A GIRL | 21

SHORE TO SHORE | 22

YOUR SWEETIES | 23

STORM AND HURRICANE | 24

QUAKE | 25

MOONSHINE | 26

MY FATHER | 28

SPRING | 29

DREAM | 32

UTTERLY | 33

YOUR MAGIC | 34

RIPENESS | 35

PURPLE DUSK | 36

APPLE OF TRANSGRESSION | 37

HER NAME IS AUTUMN | 39

SPRING AND SWALLOWS | 40

OF HEART AND LOVE | 42

GOLDEN AUTUMN | 44

NOT ALWAYS | 46

APPLE OF SIN | 47

VIOLET PETALS | 49

BROKEN PROMISE | 50

UNDER THE RAINBOW | 51

WITH SECRECY | 53

UNENDING TALE | 54

THE EASIEST | 57

PEACEFULLY | 58

CUP OF DELIGHT | 60

THE FIRST SIN | 62

HEART TO HEART | 64

MOON – BARK | 66

FAITHFULNESS | 67

TREMBLE | 68

MULTILONGING | 69

DREAM – FLIGHT | 70

DREAM GLOW | 72

OLD GUITAR TUNE | 74

WET DREAM | 75

SECRET GLOW | 77

INSPIRED | 78

LOSS | 79

YEARNING | 80

UPON THE WALKS | 81

THE MUSIC OF YOUR NAME | 82

ACCOMPLISHMENT | 83

THE MOST BEAUTIFUL GIRL | 85

DEDICATION OF WINE | 86

SUSPICION | 87

GOOD TIDINGS | 88

STARLIT | 89

INTIMATE CONVERSATION | 90

YOU ARE BEAUTIFUL | 91

EYE COLOR | 92

BETWEEN SUNRISE AND SUNSET | 94

WARM COUNTRY | 96

FROM SHOR TO SHORE | 98

THE SECRET OF GLITTER | 99

PURPLE EVENING | 100

OF HEART AND OF LOVE | 101

PEACEFULLY | 103

ENDURING FAIRY TALE | 105

WITH PRIMARY LOVE | 108

OF HEAVEN AND SEA | 111

SOUVENIR | 113

DESIRE | 115

SURVIVAL | 116

ACHIEVEMENT | 117

MASTER | 118

DESPONDENCY | 119

EMBRACE | 120

SUNDIAL | 121

INTOXICATION | 123

CONDITIONALLY | 124

AUTUMN LEAF | 125

HOT WITH LOVE | 127

LOVEFLOODED | 128

ON THE PAVEMENTS | 129

UNREACHABLE | 130

THE SWEET OF LIFE | 131

AMERICA THE THIRD WAY | 133

LOVE | 134

WITH DIFFERENCE | 135

WAITING | 136

WITH FAITH | 137

THE STAR OF DREAM | 138

THE SPRINGS AND SWALLOWS | 139

THUNDERBOLT | 141

A BEGINNING | 142

WITH OPTIMISM | 143

TATTLETALE | 144

BOYHOOD | 145

WITH THE SAME DEVOTION | 146

OF HEART AND LOVE | 147

THE THIRD HANDFUL OF EARTH | 148

WITH GUILTINESS | 150

SENTIENCE | 152

RED APPLE | 154

OF SKY AND SEA | 156

ANXIETY | 157

CHARMED WITH SECRETS | 159

OF SWAN | 160

STRIPTEASE | 162

NIGHTMARISH | 164

THE DANCER | 165

LOVE | 166

INFLAMED SUMMER | 167

FIREWORKS OF LOVE | 168

PREVALENCE | 169

CLEANED PAGE | 170

HOPE AND GLIMMER | 171

ROSES PERFUME | 173

...IN ORDER TO KISS | 175

THE SINGING ANGEL | 176

THE AMERICAN PULSE | 177

*** | 178

LOVE LINE

✿ ✿ ✿

The cricket screeches and scoffs,
The cricket squeaks and lectures,
As if inquires in the depth of the night
The deep secrets of life.

GRISH DAVTIAN

MOST DESIRED

With the reddish blossoming of the days
Your pink cheeks are glittering;
Your lips are ripe like apples;
Your breasts are filled with pomegranates;
Drunk with all such flavors
Where else can I glean your desires?

You know that I regard you
As the most desirable
For loving
With such wonderful concepts of love
Reachable in your bosom,
Reachable in my bosom,
With cuddles,
With the warmest lovemaking
And embraces . . .

You have embraced my life
With seven colors rainbow.

A smiling glance of a blessed life
Is spread all through the alter of my heart.

There are no distances
For the glimmer of sunrays;
The curves and depths
Are carved and pressed together,
With softness and warmth,
With compassion and ripeness,
Matured with satiety of desires.

Let, then,
The gulp be complete,
Without any loss of leaks;
After all the honey is squeezed from roses

Love Line

Drip by drip,
By the cherishing tentacles of honeybees...

Submerge me,
Submerge me with a complete guzzle
To be the uttermost intoxication.
Intoxicate me
From the beginning to the finish
With a permanent push,
Until the last pant,
Until final flashing...
Then let quiescence fall
On the past and future yearnings,
Earned
By wholehearted effort and belief...
Earned.
For contentment
Of many losses,
Of many longings...

Do not feel remorseful for my sacrifices,
But be proud for my heroism
By which I have sought you,
Found you
And kissed you...
Regarding you as the most desired...

Hark, there
Breaks down my logic,
Rhyme and syllables are deranged
By natural needs
So that I can endure...

From there on begins
My solemn and reserved daily.
Let me last with that,
Yet exist with you...

BETRAYAL

An exuberant genie
Inspires me the style.

My inventiveness is fruitful
And alternates
With my hereditary stupidity.

So, I go on living
And loving you
And the children
And the life . . .

And those few
Whom I keep unknown
To you.

LOVE LINE

THE OLD SONG OF GUITAR

The radio is broadcasting an old tune
The tune seems to be weeping.

When was it . . . I used to love you,
I remember it by that tune.

Now whenever it resounds
All my memories scramble.

REMINDER

You are a desirable fairy tale
To narrate.
You are a lovely song
To sing.
You are a whispering breeze
To cool down.
You are a ripe pomegranate
To strain.
You are a red apple
To bite.

You are . . .

Desire me to come.

HOT WITH LOVE

I want the flavor of your lips,
And the silkiness of your thighs,
The secret wishes of your whispers
And the turmoil in your sight.

So that you will faint in my bosom,
In the loop of my arms,
O! It is the loop of your love
Which is strangling this lover.

Your bosom, the garden of my dreams,
Is ripe with softness,
With its whiteness and tremor
It lures me to sinfulness.

In my palms is your bust
To bend and collapse on your chest,
To mix the thirst of my desires
With your secret yearnings too.

To feel your breathless panting,
The beat of your wild heart,
To rinse the foaming taste of your love,
And cool the heat of my thirst.

Prayer

Cherish me like the creator,
Dispel my sadness;
I have fallen into a deadlock,
Into interminable torments.

My glowing hopes have
Departed with my dreams;
Without leaving any rustle,
Any rosy hue.

Now it is the black and the dark
Covering my esteemed wishes;
The wings of my flight are broken
On the cliffs of calamity.

My white-breasted swallow
Came across with an evil arrow;
The ignoble fraudulent hand
Set up a snare and intrigue.

Cherish me and console me,
Put an end to this torture;
Grant hope to my heart, and illuminate,
Brighten up my dark days.

Break the conspiracy,
Break the insidious hand ten folds;
Raise the wounded swallow of my hopes
Into the heights of the blue.

So that I may achieve my aims,
Approach my creator.
Lights and hopes . . . my heart and soul
May gather strength in happiness.

Spring Night

The night has spread its dark wings
Brooding on the sleeping nature,
The mysterious silence
Of ancient times
Scatters myths in the atmosphere.

Darkness fades away
From the appearance of the moon.
The stars start blinking
Like thousands of eyes of infinity.

Thick oak trees, like silent spirits,
Standing on their shadows,
On their widespread roots,
Are watching the terrain,
Listening to the whispers of the foliage.

The moon, the lover of clouds,
Hurriedly penetrates their nuptial bed
Taking with itself the sparkling stars
As its obedient bridesmaids.

The darkness,
Thousand-headed mythical monster,
Wriggles in,
Becomes alive by a lightening,
Followed by a sky-mangling cloudburst.
Massy drops of shower hit the ground.

Lightning and thunder again,
You do not know
Whether it is the anger or the joy of nature.

After an unexpected torment
Of barely a few minutes,
The cloudburst cuts off.

Grish Davtian

A confusing spring evening
Becomes an ordinary expanse of peace.
Lovers of the nightfall
Start walking on the sidewalks.

Days on

See, the sun shines,
The moon winks,
The stars twinkle brightly
In the distances of the sky;
The long rows of the days
That have spun the length of years,
Stretch from childhood
And connect with today.

Yet in the twist of the thread,
In the folds of the years,
What a kind of life,
Made into balls of thread, twists, and folds,
And memories have bunched together.

Accumulated a sense of loss,
Sweet and burning,
With a heart beating intimacy,
And kin warmth,
With clear love and devotion,
Fervor and contribution,
Creative labor,
Campaign and victory,
A hailing here,
A face there,
A sweet glance yonder,
Touches your heart and soul,
Burns with yearning...

The heart feels squeezed, gasping,
With memories of years,
Full of the plenty of familiar expanses,
And warmth of embraces.

The roads and days
Woven together in colorful rosette
Are stretched in the blue,
From horizon to horizon,
From the distance of today
The deep nostalgia resounds
In the long and uninterrupted interval,
From home to heart,
Sweetened with feelings
With a rainbow of love.

With olden devotions,
And energetic reflections,
With merits of years,
Brimful benefices,
A meaningful life
By which the worthy forehead is decorated
With gleaming brightness,
By which the heart beats
Under the chest
With a harmonic throbbing hymn.

The old eagle with hang wings,
But still hovering in the high,
In his eyes is a saintly image
Of unreturnable past,
In his eyes is a treasured promise,
In his eyes is an old spark.

And the sun blinks,
And the moon blinks.

LOVE LINE

QUEST

In my quest
You are pictured
In line and curve,
Line and curve...

You are a shadow,
In the softness
I plunge,
I plunge...

You like it to be
Gently light
To see my paleness,
Light paleness...

The purple of the evening
Extends before me
Like your arms
In purple,
In purple...

Save me,
So that I may believe in the future,
In my devotion,
My devotion...

The lane bends
And crosses over
The little bridge.

Let us walk together,
Cross the bridge
And go away,
Far away...

OF FEELING, OF LOVE, OF DEVOTION, OF LONGING AND OF MEMORY

O, my soft songs of bygone days,
I am not longing for you at all,
I am longing for the feelings
By which I sang you.

I sang my colorful love,
My true devotion;
I am longing for that love,
And my innocent dedication.

And I turn these pages,-
Emotional soft songs
Drip from their words and lines
All longings and memories of the past.

Once Upon A Time

There was a time
When you looked at me
With awe and admiration.
The stars of your eyes glimmered.

There was a time
You smiled to me
With wishes and expectation,
The sun of your desires
Warmed me up.

You came to me
With your beauty and charm,
With your smile and sweetness,
You talked,
The music resounded.

Somehow or accidently,
With a graceful movement of your hand,
As if you wanted to cut the distance,
You patted me,
Which sent sparks through me,
Bewildered me.

Your glance deepened,
Your smile widened,
Your sentence paused . . .

I could not remember some word
To continue the conversation.

It was funny, and we chuckled,
The interruption ended
With good feelings.

GRISH DAVTIAN

> And you
> Looked,
> Smiled,
> Talked,
> And ...
> The same thing happened again.
>
> We felt good.

LOVE LINE OF WINTER

She wants to put her arms around me . . .
So she says it is cold,
Steam rises from her lips;
I reject her, I do not care,
The moment is so cruel,
I am mournful with past memories.

She, who is a whitish, beautiful girl,
Envies, and burst on to me,
Although she embraces me,
But only like a touch,
And withdraws proudly in time.

Her touch is smooth and fragile
Like the snow,
Whitish and soft girlish,
The blue of her eyes is infinite,
Where I simply get lost.

My heart feels grave . . . in the cold of winter
I fling myself . . . and nearly clasp her . . .
But she melts away like the rime of night,
Leaving her wet kiss on my lips.

I know, she melted from the grief of my rejection,
She is just a whitish, beautiful girl;
Oh, I cannot put her out of my mind,
Just like a fleeting free love.

BLAZE OF LOVE

I desire the taste of your lips and the smoothness of your thighs,
The whisper of your secret longings and the turbulence of your gaze.

So that you will swoon in my bosom, in the firm grip of my arms,
O, it is the ring of your love that strangles me.

Your bosom, the garden of my dreams, is ripe with warm softness,
With gentleness and quiver, you lead me to sins.

I wish to twist your waist and fall on your chest,
And quench the deep thirst of my desires with your desires.

I wish to breathe your breath, feel the pounding of your heart,
Wring the sweet of your love and cool the blaze of your bosom.

I will wrench the fire of my feelings into your bosom and embrace the stars,
Aggregate the echoes of your sighs in the deep sea of my heart.

INFINITY

In relation with you
The sweetness of life ripens,
Becomes enjoyment and happiness,
Tasty with bliss . . .

Flashes and illusion,
Flashes and illusions
Becomes real as
Light and warmth,
Light and warmth . . .

That is how the life becomes actual,
Which is an inexhaustible ending
Of expectations . . .

Eternity is devotion
That cannot be defined by meaning,
Or be conditioned by causality,
By cash value . . .

Plunge into my bosom,
Do not worry
With story of survival,
Because we are the convicts
Of an inexhaustible ending . . .

Ray and dew,
Ray and dew . . .
Diluted reality of concept
In the flow of time . . .

No net can now catch us,
We have reached to the freedom,
No bounds are left in our sight . . .

Grish Davtian

> Plunge into my bosom,
> Plunge into my bosom . . .
> In the softness you will not feel any fall,
> You will not reach the bottom,
> No bounds are left . . .

Spring Is A Girl

Penetrated into my heart with flowers of the garden,
She is a girl with rosy cheeks,
Spring is her name, she scents of maturity
With an open collar shirt on herself.

The hot light of her bosom pricks my eyes,
Her lips are ripe as peaches;
Her hearty love blossoms with roses,
She tells me to pick them.

So juicy . . . I relish it like a bee.
She tells me not to, as it is lethal.
I do not know whether it is death, poison, or a feast,
I feel giddy, as merry go round.

Her name is spring, she is all over my chest,
She scents like rose petals;
I feel breathless, she has thorns on her hands,
And sometimes stings severely.

But suddenly she becomes a string of beads,
Hanging from my neck, shining,
She turns all my anxieties into a deep sigh,
Throws it to the breeze and laughs.

She whispers softly to my ear and tells me,
Tells me tales of spring;
Mature girl she is with rosy cheeks,
Wearing a cheap floral shirt.

Grish Davtian

Shore To Shore

We are lost, and wander from shore to shore,
And cannot find what we are looking for.

What are we looking for, we do not know.
We do not find what we do not know from shore to shore.

Where were we born, where do we live, where will we end up?
We do not even know where we will expire from shore to shore .

Scattered like stars all around the horizon,
Where do we search for hope and the land from shore to shore .

Love Line

Your Sweeties

I want you to come and bring
Your fragrances
That feel my pitcher
With the taste of your lips;
That scorch my temples
With the cresses of your gasp;
That whispers endearment
And grant feelings to my thoughts.

I want you to come and bring
Your softness,
That awards me the pleasure
Of your lips and bosom,
And wraps around me
Your thighs,
Exhausts my boil, fever, and panting.

Come and bring your soft
And warm effeminacy,
Deep cuddles,
Your favorite sweeties I desire.

Storm And Hurricane

Your midsummer maturity is more fragrant
Than the spring bloom.

A variety of colors expand in your eyes.

Your bosom has the heat of summer
With the abundance of your pomegranates
Of your breasts,
Red wine drips from the ripe grapes of your lips.

In the deep horizon of your eyebrows
Your glance is fascinating.

Butterflies in my heart are swarming with emotions,
Flattering with frenzy to drink your aroma.

Craving to reach , to attain the sanctity of your embrace
And open the veil of my prayer.

My blood-storm is seeking the hurricane of your bosom,
With a longing to ferment and fuse.

LOVE LINE

QUAKE

How does the flower feel
When the dewdrop drips
In the heart of the flower cup
In the lovely bed of twilight . . .

It quivers probably
With a love felt feverish fever.

That is how I feel
When I embrace you by my glance . . .

MOONSHINE

There was you,
There was the night,
And there was I.

There was no whisper,
It was your breath,
Which was a murmur
Of the breeze.

There was a star,
May be a meteor,
It was your eyes
Which were shining
By the sparks of your desires,
My desires . . .

You were hot,
You were scorching,
Putting on fire.

Your tears were soft
In your misty glance.

My lips caressing your lips,
Beautiful,
Honey taste.

In the moonshine
The tale was whispering
A secret story
In the melody of your mutters.

I desire
The new moon
Be your eyebrows.

Love Line

Shadows were gathering
With passion.

I was flashing with temperature,
Flirting.

There were us,
There was the moon.

Our shadow on the earth,
I had become you.

My Father

I miss my father
When I am a grateful father myself,
When standing around me are
My children with loving hearts.

My children are in my loving heart
I retain my home with their breath,
Just as he was doing it
With the secret tradition of our forefathers.

My children are in my loving heart,
My love is the heart of my home,
Like the sun in the sky
With the song of my life.

He was at the threshold of our home,
Together with his love, my mother,
With their live breath
Upheld our home full of joy . . .

And I am standing strong, too,
Arm in arm with my wife,
Together with the total fortune of my children,
As father and mother
We have become a home of our own.

He was like a steadfast pillar
Holding our sacred ceiling high
On his shoulders of endeavor,
In the heart of his devoted love . . .

And my house is stable too,
And my faith is the Lord, my God,
His grace is unending
Filling my home with blessings.

SPRING

You arrive in her fresh footsteps,
Through the twirling and flowing path,
From where she has passed with light steps,
But has sunk into my heart
As a warm and bright ray,
That flows with my blood,
With feeling and harmony,
Whirl-pooling, deepening,
Deepening.
And from the depths of my heart
Sprouts like lit blossom,
With the good tidings of the awaking nature,
As a blue flower
Which is a bright shred of a dream,
A heartening promise
Lingering under the sun,
Breathing with her scent,
Caressing my temples,
Smearing her warmth on my lips
With a yearning of my kisses.

You arrive with her finicky gait,
Twisting her thin waist,
Avoiding my embrace,
Like the cloud, which clasps to the moon
But slips from the crescent,
And piles up like the solemn dreams of my frown.

You arrive through those remote roads
From where my dreams pass
With irretrievable memories,
Spinning the secret story of my life
With dramatic fascination;
Through the pastures of my desires,
Where my needs graze

Grish Davtian

Like innocent lambs.
My desires exult like butterflies,
On whose wings you arrive.

You arrive with her thrill
And enter my heart.

I worship your flowering,
The petals of which
She sprinkled on my chest
As compassion and happiness.
I worship your narcissi
With gold cups
Full of dew, by which
The nightingales of my whishes got drunk,
Warbling ode to her.
I worship your violets,
Your white jasmines,
By which you are ornamented
And thus resembling her,
Become worthy of my adoration.

With the peace of the mornings
Inseminate my desires,
So that in my supplication
I may feel the taste of her kisses;
Admire her beauty
With assurance of my loyalty
And feel my dedication
With the warmth of my love,
By which you arrive with a renewed life,
You arrive unchanged as continuation,
And grant taste and scent,
As lasting copiousness,
As meaningful returns of solemn departures.

LOVE LINE

You arrive,
Enter my heart,
And flourish.

Dream

Clear and temperamental night,
Lunar light crashing all around,
Grant me to embrace her
In my arms,
And feel her heartbeat,
Her tenderness and devotion.

The soft breeze of her breath
Touches my temples,
In the silence of the moment
I squeeze the cherries of her lips.

Let her eyes blink through fancy dreams,
Let me steal delight from her bosom,
With fervent desire
Warming my heart,
Granting her yearning.

In life
Every creature has
His share of wishes.

That is fair and good,
Decorated with lush and plush.

Clear and temperamental night
Feast over the moonshine
And sparkling stars.

LOVE LINE

UTTERLY

The rainbow is colored by my love
That I wrap around your shoulders.

The vibrations of my feelings
Are wonderful marvels of nature
That I award to you
In the warmth of my arms,
In the pavilion of my bosom.

The throb of my drunkenness
Expands with a magic tale,
While the twilight of tranquility
Fades with radiance and glow.

You look at me
With the ponds of your eyes
Which become the sea of your gaze,
And your smile shines like stars.

I want to whisper words in your ears,
Only for you,
But my mind does not envision
The meaning of what I am seeking.

It is without any sense and reason
That I am dedicated to you.

That is why
I have no size and measure,
I am devoted to you entirely.

Your Magic

It is only you
With the touch of magic
Which make me tremble
When you on my lap,
And my clasp.

It is only you
And your magic.

RIPENESS

This year
Autumn has exploded in blond,
It has exploded in red;
Autumn has smeared
A puff of cloud
On my hair and beard,
Autumn has sprinkled
A pinch of salt
To sweeten my life.

Your cheeks have turned red
Like the dawns and
Like the sunsets;
Your cheeks have turned red.
But the twist
By which you twirl your waist
Is in the ring of my arms . . .
In the ring of my arms . . .

A warmth flashes through my palms,
I desire to feel your touch
From which I shivered that night . . .
I shivered . . .

There is warmth in my palms now,
There is warmth in my temples now,
My heart is pounding
In your warm bosom.

My devotion is colorful in blond,
Your devotion is sparkling in red;
Autumn has flared up in ripeness . . .
In ripeness . . .

Grish Davtian

Purple Dusk

The horizon of sunset is clear purple,
The mountains are purple and smooth like ruby.

When I look at the sunset, and look into your eyes,
I turn to those days of vain and sweet dreams . . .

To those delicate days that were in the same purple color,
Kindling my wistful love of faraway places.

They were full of warmth, youth, and simplicity,
And what I call with repentance as madness . . .

With a madness that erupts from sacred devotion,
Creating love and purity distilled from unadulterated gold.

Those emotions, deep feelings touch my heart,
Connect me to the world and resound.

They resound and clink with melancholy of good old memories
In the distance of the horizon . . . purple and cloudless . . .

LOVE LINE

APPLE OF TRANSGRESSION

You are a sparkling dream,
Appeared in my life
Created a celebration
Yet you are not in the arena.

That is a pretty comedy,
A clever eyewash,
With such a dept
Deprived of fascination.

You are an exquisite butterfly,
With golden, delicate wings,
As a glitter of the sunbeam,
Enchanting flirtation.

Your lips are as cherry and apricot,
As the apple of transgression;
Your bosom is a paradise of love,
The tranquility of cohabitation.

You will not . . . you will not endure
When I touch you with desire;
You will melt like a candle
Burning with light.

Come . . . with all your elegance,
Sophistication and grace,
With your rich flavorsome ripeness,
And the fire of your desires.

I will take you to the blue,
In the colors of the rainbow;
I will decorate your way,
I will squeeze the pomegranate of your love.

Grish Davtian

You will reach to your pure intoxication,
The torpor of inebriation,
With my viral magic
In the depth of Milky Way.

HER NAME IS AUTUMN

A blond lass is waiting on my path,
With humid lips, barefoot,
Her braided hair in the breeze, topless, thin,
I like her, her name is Autumn.

I call her, and she holds me in her arms,
Fills the pits of my path with fallen leaves,
Wets my lips with the rain,
Whispers to my ear, that her name is Autumn.

I want to take her home as my bride,
To care for me and to love me,
To cuddle me at night in her warm bosom,
To tell me she loves me,
To tell me that her name is Autumn.

Blond Autumn . . . blond Autumn.
Oh, my colorful memories . . .
Fallen and scattered in my heart
Like roses and thorns . . .
I want her every day and night . . .
And cannot forget that her name is Autumn . . .

Grish Davtian

Spring And Swallows

There are springs,
which have their own swallows,
that melodize
the year, the time,
which is the life.

Life has its melody,
its song,
that sounds like a bell,
hung in our school.

Its clink
has a note of fortune
and I like it.

It is with the same feelings
that I draw bells
on the New Year's greeting cards.

I ring the melody of fortune,
that starts at our school
and spreads,
reaches us and our time,
we enter the classroom
which is the life.

The swallows are chirping
building a nest .

. It is us,
Falling in love
going to secret dates
and getting the taste .

Love Line

Forming our family,
Melodizing the music
with loud notes,
by point in time and hour,
which is the life.

Life has its breeze,
that whispers in our garden,
in the yard of our school
and caresses trees and flowers
and roses,
that are more aromatic
than a dream .

.Trees and flowers and roses:
our assets.

Those are our thoughts.
our wishes,
our emotions,
our loves.

.That we enjoy throughout the time,
which is the life
melodized,
resounding
and muttering.

It is with all these
that I love the swallows,
that I love the spring.

GRISH DAVTIAN

OF HEART AND LOVE

I am chatting
With good opportunities for well-being,
As the arch of rainbow
Connects together
The present and the future.

The good news rings
And my desires heat up
As the furnace of my heart and love...
My heart and love...

I know the stars in the sky
Spout
From the furnace of heart and love,
They scatter in the sky and our bosoms
Fertile with hope and kindness...

We are involved with the world,
In the blue of the constellation,
In each other's arms,
With illumination
In the lights...

It is flooded with lights
Present and future
With new possibilities...

I bend on the anvil and hammer,
I tear off stars,
That are as hot as my dreams,
Like my heart
And like my love,
Like you...

Love Line

I decorate you with the sparks of my heart
And the stars of my love,
To stay warm and desirable...
Hot and desirable...

Golden Autumn

I never loved you,
Yet I eulogized you often,
Golden Autumn
Of nature
And my life;
Yet, you always
Scattered in my pathway
Your withered leaves,
And your abundant fruits,
Ripe and delicious.

If I never had
The blossoming of the spring
With its torrent of warmth;
The original instinct, holy and creative,
To love and to possess;
If I never had the heat of the summer,
And the charge which boils my blood;
If I never had ...
I would have worshipped your gold,
The harvest of all those experiences
I stored day by day in the tower of my years,
Becoming full, conscious, and thoughtful.

If I never had
The stipulate conception of super pursuits
Of the swift world,
Exploding, waning, reviving, crumbling,
Conquering
Every moment;
If I never had
My inherited flame of my earthly gene,
From superstring atom
Of the great chaos,
Creator and destroyer;

LOVE LINE

If I never had.
Oh, then,
I would never have been that bee
Who lived
With the fiery passion to possess the flowers;
That dew
To clasp to the petals of roses with coolness;
That breeze that combs the skulls of the peaks.
I would never have been,
I would never have been what I am.

Golden autumn,
Golden autumn,
I never loved you;
Although I mold your gold,
Although I dedicate my songs
To the sprouting and blossoming of spring,
To the assured swooping maturity,
Filled with the warmth of summer
With the strength of pleasured bequeathal.

And now,
In the golden stall of your abundance,
Anointed with the ripeness of the sun,
And violet rays of distant,
From whence to wherever
Ascending with decent dignity,
With intentional aim,
And with irreproachable and virile dissatisfaction,
Golden autumn,
Let me not remain indebted to you.

Not Always

It is not always that I talk in the words of my heart,
It is because of my mind, I judge by my thoughts,
I measure, weigh by the experience of my life,
Which is the field where I have sawn and have harvested.
Nevertheless,
I am not always enriched by the yields of my mind.

Apple Of Sin

You are a bright dream
Appeared in my life
Created a celebration
Yet you are not in the show.

It is a beautiful tale,
Smart and eye washing,
Salty in taste
Confusing in detail.

You are a delicate and colorful butterfly
With golden wings and fragile,
Like a sunbeam
Enchanting loveplay.

Your lips are like cherry and apricot,
Like the apple of sin,
Your bosom is the embrace of love,
And peace of cohabitation.

You cannot . . . you will not endure
If I touch you with desire,
You will melt like a candle
Burning in fire.

Come with all your graceful coquetry
And charming philandering,
With your sweet tastefulness
And with the fire of desires and lust.

I will take you to the blues,
With the colors of rainbow,
I will decorate your path
And will squeeze your pomegranate with love.

Grish Davtian

I will deliver you to puberty,
Drunkenness and somnolence,
With my manly magic
In the deeps of the Milky Way.

VIOLET PETALS

She is a verdurous flower with violet petals,
She is a tender girl, scenting like a violet,
On her honeyed lips are words of love,
And in her honey-colored eyes are violet dreams.

She has arrived with longings of distant lands,
And has perched in the warm depths of my heart,
She is showering on me petals of violet,
Narrating for me stories of heart and love.

There has been a day rising with the sun of youth,
And a happy youngster wandering in the garden,
Who used to catch butterflies and was fascinated with colors,
But kept his secrets of what he felt.

He has kept in his memories the glitter of her eyes,
By which he was struck and singed.
She is now flitting about in his front,
But he is unable to catch her with his trembling fingers.

I am trembling with the shiver of admiration and love,
I am bristling up by the love of my youth days.
She is a tender girl, scenting like a flower,
She is showering on me petals of violet.

BROKEN PROMISE

They all promised to my loving heart.

The sun promised to rise
And paint the day with light.

The moon promised to renew always
And shave the chin of the night
With the sharp edge of the crescent.

The stars promised to glitter
And spray dews to the fiery flowers,
To wet the tows of the breeze
When it touches the petals.

You promised to my loving heart.

Your eyes promised your love;
Your lips promised to extinguish
My flames with kisses.

And although the sun rises
And paints the day with light;
The moon renews and slides
With the light-and-dark patterns;
The stars glitter proudly,
Dews fall on the petals of roses
Wetting the lips of the breeze.

Yet all your given promises remain
As the passing melody of words only.

My desire seeks you with a rustle
But do not reach to your guilty kisses.

Under The Rainbow

All the colors that you have scattered in my heart
Have colored the tale
In this best expanse of my life's novel.
I have braided this beautiful rainbow
With soul admiring love song
Which charmingly resembles
Your silhouette.

The velvet of a cloud covers the sun,
The gilded vivid bunch of rays
Unravels with a chilly rain shower,
Cools down my thirst,
For which I praise God,
Yet discontented for remaining indebted to you.

Do become plentiful of love,
Make me breathless
With density of colors.

Then the mist of the cloud dissipates,
The sun becomes like your warmth,
Awards me with breath and soul,
Rewards me with rest.

Now fill me,
Christen me with the seal of your citizenship,
So that I will remain under your belonging
By conviction, but not by captivity.

By this wonderful play of sun and rain
Behold the rainbow I have braided
With intentional willingness,
And with heartfelt gladness
I am hanging it from your neck,
I am wrapping it around your shoulders,

Grish Davtian

So that you will remain
Unsurpassed ornament
In the altar of my heart.

LOVE LINE

WITH SECRECY

The sunset of autumn wrings
Tears of the clouds on my pale face
with scent;
What past sins am I expiating
That gives me such heartbeat?

It is a shred of a secret story:
That you looked for the first time,
That I stayed indifferent witness,
And your glance broke away reluctantly.

A play of light and shadow:
That I did not realize you desired me.
Illusion of a mad dreamer
Which is still clear as an innocent imagination.

A voice is rising from the depth of my longing
Whining in my solitude;
What unrepented sin am I expiating
Secretly kept in my heart.

Unending Tale

In the warm days of this late summer
My heart is filled
With cool desires of an early spring,
So that you would come to me
With immaculate love of youth,
As was the dew on the petals of flower,_
So with that ancient feeling,
Which was new to me,
Which was love,
Or was not,
Perhaps it was true love,
Which I was newly finding in my life,-
To hold your hand
And pull you to me,
Your breasts would bump to my proud chest,
I should look into the depth of your eyes,
As if into the clear lake of the mirror,
Where always, always
I used to feel warmer,
I used to melt you more,
You used to become mine submissively,
With purified nakedness,
With cleanness of love.

In these warm days of late summer
My cool desires of this sparkling spring
Are heaving abundantly,
I possess you with earned devotion,
Which has cultivated the sweat
Of diligence of my faithfulness.

You are fresh and delicate,
Budding,
And it suffices me to touch you,
With the sure strength of holy creation,

LOVE LINE

You bloom abruptly with colorful flowers
To fill my spring and my summer
With the glory of beauty and delight
That the suns never denied me
In the dispersions of diasporas,
But endowed me with your kisses,
And your entire caresses.

Do hover in my heart
Which is, perhaps, the greater part of this world
With the clear intensity of blue sky;
No rose has ever withered there,
But has sprouted with noble scent,
Even for a while,
Until you have given it a fresh start,
And the start is always like a complete spring.

The mornings are colorful and fresh,
Fly with me
With the flight of my interrupted dream,
The shred of which is still on my eyelids
And the blue tale of my world
Has no ending.

In the warm days of this late summer
My cool desires of an early spring
Carry the vessel loaded with flowers
To the remoteness of the blue sea of my shore-less heart,
Where you reign imperiously
Embracing the oars of love and hope,
Where you have dipped yourself in the clear craving,
Reaching to the depths of my delights too,
Which have no ending
Like the tales of my emotions.

This fine tale of my deep wishes
Sweetened with the aroma of summer and spring
Still tastes on my tongue

With the oozing sweetness of your kisses
And have no ending.

Love Line

THE EASIEST

She was evaluating my shyness.

She asked:
What would you do
If I suddenly appear
In front of you
Naked!

I said:
I will shut my eyes
So
You would not feel
Ashamed.

She liked it so much
That undressed.

It had never happened
So easily.

Peacefully

The peace you bring me
Is like the ripple-sway of the field,
Which snatches me out of exhausting anxieties,
Takes me to the seclusion of my soft wishes,
Close to my heart,
Like my desire.
That you embrace me with pure happiness
Endow me the honey and wine of love
With total plush taste of your lips.

Hug me strongly
So my anxieties will be strangled in the loop of your arms;
Cover my neck with myriad kisses,
Press your palms to my burning temples
And spread your bosom on my chest.

That which is ripening with devotion
Let last long as the chime,
Which shudders me causing gooseflesh,
Which has a mad hop of teens,
Crashes with the dispersion of a wave,
And calms down with ebbing,
Panting with deep breath,
Exhausting tiredness.

Bring peace to my struggling soul,
To enjoy the victory of love,
To acquire the instinct of belonging,
And cherish you with content in my realm.

Now with heartfelt desires
I am yielding to your carrying sways;
With a sacred loyalty of a unique wish
I am taking you in my arms,
Flying and taking you

LOVE LINE

Beyond the arch of the rainbow
Woven in seven colors,
To the colorful world of love.

Breathe my breath,
So that I may inhale you with insemination,
To bloom lilies in the kernel of your heart,
And open the blue secret of the life;
With reconciled peace
Reward you with my tranquility
In the azure deep of the horizon,
Which you regaled me serenely.

The peace that you present me
Is like the calm wave of the field,
Like the calm wave.

Cup Of Delight

You, the woman of my blazing desires,
Sun-kissed and beautiful,
Like a sparkling rose of perfumes,
Flowering flower, colorful butterfly,
I can catch you in the warmth of my arms,
You are desirable like a blue edged dream,
A crystal cup of delight and joy.

Do approach me with abundance of luck
From the distances of despair,
From the cold frosts of heights
And fall into my arms,
Bright with the taste of the sun,
And quench my craving
With the richness of your splendid presence.

Grant me your life supporting warmth
With unobtrusive elegance,
With unprejudiced liking and love,
As our pagan and fertile grandmas did
Satiating our love hungry granddads.
Grant me your ripe maturity and softness,
So, my heart will become fruitful
With apples of paradise,
Which turn reddish
As the rosy cheeks of Eve.

Let me enjoy your purity pink,
Drink the honey of your lips,
Kiss your swan like gracious neck,
Rinse the lush abundance of your breasts,
To give you the pleasure of feeling loved.

Your amiable freshness would not last,
As with the spring and summer

Love Line

There come withering of autumn,
The frost and cold of winter.

Before fading of autumn
And the chill of winter
Pour into my arms.
Although I cannot deliver you,
But I will make your spring bloom,
I will fertilize your summer
With abundance of memories,
With the nectar of lust and desire.
The murmur of my melody will take you
Far away to shores of marvels and miracles,
Your dreams will all come true.

Sun-kissed and beautiful woman of my desires
Pour into the cup of my pleasures
The wine of your sweetness
To toast my admiration of your satisfaction
To toast to your happiness,
Free-will and agreement.

THE FIRST SIN

With dreams of violet hue
And with panting of wistful memories
I remember
That awesome mystery night of the old, decrepit village.

The golden sun shrouded its rays
In the blushing west,
The dark throng of shredded shadows
Arrived without any melody.
The thin black veil
With flights of delicate dreams
Censed sleep
From the eaves of steep roofs.
In the expanding shroud of the pale moonlight
The weary village fell asleep with blue thoughts.

Sacred promises in our hearts
We walked through the waves of newly plowed fields
To the ruined cathedral,
To kiss the stone-crosses there.

The shadows stretched out along our way
Like fire worshiping majestic priests.

We knelt down in the courtyard of the stone-crosses
To offer our sacred prayers,
Sacred and bright prayers,
Dedicated to each other,
While holding our secret love as an altar
In the innocence of our hearts.

The illusive phantoms of heavenly, vain saints
Flocked around us
Scared of our divine prayers.
While the spirits soared gently above us

Love Line

We concluded our prayers and vows,
And kissed the stone-crosses in the courtyard.

But there was one stone-cross standing vehemently tall,
Holding high its proud and smooth forehead,
That we could not kiss.
You implored and I helped you up,
You embraced and kissed the stone-cross,
Yet, I remained there below
Deprived from the blessing of the unattainable kiss
Of that stone-cross.

Then you slid down. On our way back
When we sat by the spring,
I plucked the kiss of that cold stone-cross from your warm lips.

I wish. I wish I had lost my faith in the old, ruined cathedral,
So that with the thoughts of that stone-cross
I would not contaminate our pure emotions and feelings.

Heart To Heart

When I am gone
And you desire
The warmth of my love,
Go to the garden on a sunny day
As a visitor to the flowers
That I have sowed wholeheartedly
On the pages of my emotions;
The fresh blossoms of my songs will give
The scent of love
To your desires.

Even if far away
I will be close to you in love,
In the blue horizon,
In the ether.

There was an old, faraway street
We walked through it so often,
I am keeping an insignificant memory of it,
So close to my heart,
Though slightly dusty,
Yet ornamented
With your sweet glances.

It was a fortune, or was not,
But it was a life
Full of charms and lovability,
That will last even differently
If cut short by old age.

It has been achieved by maturity,
And is not measured by time.

LOVE LINE

A mixture of light and dark,
With the capacity of horizon,
As the capacity of your emotions,
Of my emotions scented with roses.

Open the pages of my love
With warmth and softness,
Hold tight to your bosom,
Like I embraced you,
Whisper my words,
The story of our love,
That weaved the happiness of our life
In numerous colors of beauty
And chimed in our hearts.

It was a life, a song,
A desirable devotion.

Grish Davtian

Moon – Bark

Dream is oozing from the censer of the moon,
A blue delusion;
Foam is chewing moss in the lagoon,
Lukewarm and humid.

In the golden ray of the moon a shadow stirred,
A sleepwalker bastard;
The breeze scattered from the folds of the dark
Gravel and sand.

The sky is turned over the earth,
Seizing sparks;
Sparkling stars gleaming faraway,
My dazzling wishes.

I wish to bend over your bosom with love,
Let the flash break out;
In our hearts, in the whole universe
Ferment will erupt.

And the azure horizon fluctuates,
Falls into slumber;
Is it a dream of a sleepwalker, or a nightmare?
Howls in the dark.

Its jaws against the silver of the moon
The dog barks;
My ardent ardor, your Milky Way bosom,
Your panting, the rustle.

FAITHFULNESS

The sea moans in the tranquility of the azure night,
Heaping its fluid back in the lights of the shore;
The pure flames wriggle and break like crystal,
Floating with the whisper of playful numerous waves.

With an infinite meaning the sea moans from depths,
That has underlined a gold-color mysticism in my life;
The stars, which are born from my eyes and wishes,
Are scattered in the blue atmosphere,
And are as sparks in my heart.

So many breezes caressed the wide sea of my bold forehead,
Caressed the longing of my eyes, with the illusions of afar;
With the shreds of my fiery thoughts, which are these whole clouds,
Sacrificed the virginity of the horizon imperturbably.

They are silent now. And I am silent, too, with the total of my words,
I have kneaded them with the taste and bloom of life and corn;
My wishes are forming up, the sea is moaning fathomlessly,
Pounding the shores of the past and of the present.

Love is exceptional. And the flames burn the darkness
At the littoral of the sea and land as sacrifice and devotion;
As fantasy, as desire flashing to the close,
On life, on fortune as giggle and vow.

As if I do not exist. But my wishes do exist and will remain so,
They will become immortal like light, in the distance of my sight,
In the colossal mixture of earth and water, storm, and fire,
By which my lips smile, by which my heart is faithful.

GRISH DAVTIAN

TREMBLE

How does the flower feel
When a dew drop
Drips into the heart of the flower cup
In the warm bed of the dusk?

It probably trembles
With the warm flood of climax.

I feel the same way
When I (squeeze) you by my glance.

MULTILONGING

In reality I wandered excessively,
Stayed here and there protracted,
Made friends and became settled,
Yet suddenly roved about again.

Wherever I stayed I loved wholeheartedly,
And was loved by so many too;
But, what happened, did a breeze blow abruptly
And separated me from my loved ones?

Yet by leaving and going away
I took my loves with me in my heart;
I took with me their loves, memories, and affections,
Those have become my deep longings.

And now, wherever I may be,
Around me and in my bosom are my loved ones,
But in my heart is my longing of those
Who are far away, who are not in my arms.

Dream – Flight

What a nice dream it was;
As if I was in our court.
Then I was riding a white horse.
Was it a horse. Was it you?
I was caressing you.
Perhaps it was a horse, and I was riding.

I was galloping fast like lightening,
I was flying in the clouds.
All neighbors were looking at me,
They were saying
"Look at him, he is the white equestrian
Flying like the lightening."
They were gossiping:
"Look, he is the stupid guy in love
Who flies in his dreams."

As if it were our vineyard,
I was eating off the vine trees,
The grapes were ripe and sweet.
Or were your lips
I was kissing.
Ripe they were. sweet they were.

My father and brother were watering the vineyard.
As if I was falling from the vine trees.
But you were reaching down and catching me,
You were touching me with desire.
We were embracing.
We embraced.
We were flying
We were so light.
I was carrying you away.

Love Line

It was a flight.
It was a quiver.
You were vibrating.
You were my vibration.

Dream Glow

It was a dream.
It was blue, it was azure.
As if I was in my room.
I was wondering why the door was not there!
The closet was there,
And my big mirror was there
With its semicircular header.

It was a blue evening of warm summer.
The sun had swung towards West,
Reflecting in the mirror.
I was standing in the reflection
And caressing the sunrays.
Perhaps I was caressing your hips.

I just pushed myself up.
And I was flying up the sunrays.
I was curling around your hips.
As if it was sunrays.
As if it was you.
I was just pushing myself up.
Like I was flying.
As if I was embracing you.
Curling around you.
As if getting absorbed deeper.

It was blue, it was azure.
It was a blue evening of warm summer.
I was in my room.
There were my books. there were you.
At my desk I was writing my poems,
Dedicating to you.
You were glowing.

Love Line

I was writing on the glow.
I was so light,
I was flying.

My mother was calling me
To have my tea.

GRISH DAVTIAN

OLD GUITAR TUNE

*Translated from Grish Davtian
by Diana Der-Hovanessian
from Armenian*

Just an old tune
played by guitar
from the radio
of a passing car,

an old song from a far-
off you and I,
stirring up the past
as the tune floats by.

WET DREAM

You came into my dream
With your same charm
And magic,
As if you were embracing me in the heavens.
You were kissing me with flirtations.
It seemed as if you were moving away.
Yet it seemed as if I was catching you.
Then the same play was repeating,
I was catching you and kissing you.
You were laughing.
I was envying you.

And then again you were running away.
Your pink skirt was waving.
Your full hips were vibrating.
As if my hands had embraced your hips,
And were burning,
And were caressing.
Close to my ear was the whisper of your breath.
I was feeling your warmth.

Then it seemed we were going away.
Then as if we entered from a door,
But there was no room, nothing behind the door,
So we jumped,
And we were flying.

You were looking straight into my eyes.
Your eyes were big and shiny.
Honey-color they were.

Then you were rubbing yourself to me deliberately.
And I was desiring you strongly.
You were rubbing yourself to me.

Grish Davtian

> You were rubbing yourself to me.
> And I was feeling your whole softness.
>
> O. I was sweating. I was in a wet dream.

SECRET GLOW

You are pretty and beautiful, or you are not,
I do not know; I do not care which one you are not;
Yet on your face, in your eyes, on your lips
There is a smile that attracts my soul.

It is a glow, a smile, a wink,
It has no relation with pretty or beauty,
It is a spark of a magic that allures me,
Relates with my feelings wholeheartedly.

The days, the sidewalks, the seashore
All are fascinating with their cute beauty;
There is the pretty, the beautiful, and the charm,
Yet the glow remains in your endowment alone.

The glow remains only in your sight,
Connected with numerous secrets and gossips,
And the days of our life, the sidewalks, and the seashore
Guard closely, properly, faultlessly.

But you do not seem to believe me,
My whisper breaks down in silence.
Whereas it is the same glow that slightly
Flashes in your sight with love.

While the tale of pretty and the beauty is not a legend.
I wonder.
Do you know? Do I not know? How then.
I seem to be grasping the secret of the glow.

Inspired

The harp of my life is resounding now with fascination,
Granting delights to my heart and soul;
The ominous tune of sadness, pain, and longing is no more,
That used to cut my breath short whenever remembered the past.

It is a mild, blonde autumn; the sun is a handful of gold
Scattered on my path, which takes me to the home of my hopes;
My car is cruising fast, without feeling
That has grown older, together with me, yet remaining the same crazy.

I will soon arrive at the garage of my old house,
I will announce my arrival by ear-piercing honk;
I will read the word of satisfaction on the sight of my beloved,
I will have my share of bread and butter with a clear conscience.

Thus I am taking my exit on the freeway
That takes me to the street close to my heart;
The forthcoming years seem to me delightful
Which inspire me with energy and grant me flying wings.

Loss

Light and dark,
Light and dark,
It is dusk;
The night is, is not discernible.

He barely passes the lane,
Turns the bent,
Reaches the dream;
It is so good,
It is so sweet,
His wishes are realized.

Dark and light,
Dark and light,
It is twilight,
The morning is, is not discernible.

Finally the light increases,
Twilight melts in the light;
The dream disappears.

He stops,
Returns,
Passes the bent,
Seeks the dream.

It is morning,
There is no dream left.

Yearning

By Grish Davtian
Translated by Knarik O. Meneshian
From Armenian

Upon these far away shores
A deep yearning
Nudges my heart
For a distant shore...

Yet now, upon these shores...
It is not that shore that is distant...
But rather
My heart...

And far is that shore,
Close to my heart,
The heart of my fiery yearning,
Oh, so far from my embrace...

My yearning is deep, it is deep...deep...

LOVE LINE

UPON THE WALKS

By Grish Davtian
Translated by Knarik O. Meneshian
From Armenian

Countless memories tumble
Upon the walks,
Like withered leaves
Upon the walks.

Snow descends and so does night
Covering the walks,
And covering old memories
Upon the walks.

Grish Davtian

The Music Of Your Name

Your name is sweet music to my ears,
That stirs me and vibrates my heart.
Like a field, I thirst for your purling,
To flower with plentiful colors.

The blushing moon slides up
Imitating your gliding steps
Passing through the web of my love,
Your pretty feet become dewy
And I realize the extent of my love
For you.

It is after so many tears
That love becomes crystallized,
Becomes dews,
Otherwise, it would have rimed,
And you would have chilled in abandoned roads.

It is the fire of love that evaporates the rime
And the dew drops on your way as a smile
Decorate your way with a grand promise,
Joining with your faith and goodness.

I always see stars in your eyes,
Your glance always reflects stars;
Bright rays are beams of light
Reverberating in the horizon.

How is it that you fill my heart with such love?
So I love you when the day breaks, the night falls;
The morning breaths into me hopes,
And the music of your name resounds.

LOVE LINE

ACCOMPLISHMENT

Whenever you look at me
And you are brimming with desire,
The mania hits on the sunny side of my heart,
I become warm
Like a piece of rock,
And I shine with smoothness,
I shine.

Whenever you put your hand on my chest,
Your palm fills with my warmth,
By which you become sweeter
Like the ripeness of late autumn.

We feel torrid,
We feel torrid,
And gasp breathlessly.

Do not worry,
This heat will not melt me,
I will sustain enough.

You dispose of yourself into my arms
And let my sultry deluge you,
Deluge you.

The ripple flies us
Over the summits of frenzy.

I need to have the power
To cleave all the bonds,
To present you satisfaction and peace.

With all our human imperfections
It is by love
That we achieve the perfection of creation,

Grish Davtian

Totally clean and bare,
With holy devotion,
By which we are discharged,
And recharged,
And become completed with satisfaction,
We become complete.

THE MOST BEAUTIFUL GIRL

I have found the most beautiful girl in the world;
In the sun of her eyes her clean glance shines,
In the curve of her warm lips there are no sins of kisses
And she promises me alone her first kiss.

I love the most beautiful girl of the world,
In the depth of her heart the sea of love swings,
In her soul of devotion is her final sacred promise,
I carve her image in the altar of my heart.

I take the most beautiful girl of the world
Through the golden path of my dreams.
The dawn and the future of my and her fiery love
Is arched and knotted together with the colorful rainbow.

I embrace the most beautiful girl of the world
With my deepest love, with my warmest desires,
By which my world lives, and my hopes are unending,
And the pigeon of my fortune hovers in the bright sky.

GRISH DAVTIAN

DEDICATION OF WINE

My heart as a chalice of love, my love as red wine in it,
I am raising my full glass to you, my home people.

With the cherished sacred traditions of Navasard
I drink to your life with fiery good wishes.

Whenever any destructive clouds clashed with you
You endured like the giant of Sassoon of lightening saber,

You stretched out your mighty hand with a heroic victory
And firmly snatched the sun from the midst of darkness.

And you shall nail the sun on the summit of Ararat,
Your own fiery sun full of the new spirit of new life.

My heart like an incombustible burning raspberry bush,
My love as the inextinguishable flame on its branch,
I drink to your sacred life, my people, my Armenians.

LOVE LINE

SUSPICION

You have drawn the map,
I am only tracing the boarders.

Invasion into the expanses
I am not allowing myself,
Just to keep in harmony
With your intention,
Which is intruding into feelings.

I wish not to define
Since secrecy has its attractions.

But it is hurting me now
In a big way.

In a way you know.

I wish not to describe.

You do not want to hurt me,
Do you?

GOOD TIDINGS

I will appear in your thoughts with my songs
Dedicated to our love
By which I placed a ring on your finger with a promise,
With a flower of a rainbow on your forehead.

Even if I be beyond the seas
I will leave my heart with you;
Even if there be storm and lightening,
I will come to your bosom
Over the mountains and through the ravines.

Clouds are gathered, my dream is confused,
I cannot see the bottom of the abyss,
Yet in my high endeavors is my purpose,
My path takes me to the summit.

The digger dug a pitfall in his base depths
And himself is at the bottom of the pit,
The moon of our fortune sweeps through the sky
It will not fall in the pitfall.

Stars are shining and the moon is bright,
The story of my dream is clearing up,
In the blue azure my hopes are afloat
Giving us good tidings of the life.

STARLIT

When did your golden teen pass,
And you became such youthful noble,
With reliable dreams and aspirations
To dedicate songs of my wishes to you.

To expand the clear blue of my love
To become the starlit sky of my belief,
To spread my wishes among the stars
Realizing them with good fortune.

It is a sunny grace of providence
Satiated with your sight and spirit,
Which is colorful with impeccable beauty.
And has been blessed by God reigning in my heart.

Do feel the seething of the family blood
That I have endowed you with secret inheritance,
There is life and secret light of goodness in your days,
Do enjoy and take delight with purpose and unshakeable will.

And do light up your own light of new life
And add your own star to the sky,
Keep the glitter of my star in your star
And pass it on to your starlit son.

Intimate Conversation

Since I have observed you often in silence
And have been in communion with your heart in silence,
You think I have lived an easy life,
And have not associated with anxiety and sorrow.

Yet, often, when I have held your hand
Pulling you as if by compulsion into my arms,
I have wished not to wear out your patience,
An aching heart cannot be cured by reminding the pain.

Yet, often, when I have said: Do not ask, as it will be fine.
And I have not had the patience to elaborate,
I have wished to encourage you in your endeavors
To earn back my losses.

I will light up the new starlets of your heart
To glitter with the sense of your satisfaction,
In order to eliminate the sorrows of both of us
The way the moon scatters the darkness.

LOVE LINE

YOU ARE BEAUTIFUL

I love you,
I flood out my feelings
That shine in my heart.

You are warm with love,
You crumble my feelings into pieces
From which sparks scatter
Everywhere.

That is how the stars appear.

The sky is full of stars.

Star-covered sky is more beautiful.

You are more beautiful
With your twin stars of eyes
Beaming on to me.

Eye Color

Your eyes,
My eyes
What color are they, my dear?

In this light,
In this darkness,
Your eyes,
My eyes,
They are the color of love,
Love-color, my dear . . .

In this hotbed of lovemaking
Do not ask
Your eyes,
My eyes
What color are they, dear . . .

Your eyes,
My eyes
They are the color of fire,
Flaming, ablaze,
They are the color of sparks,
They are sparkling, dear.
They are colorful
In the seven colors of the rainbow,
Beloved.

At this crazy moment of lovemaking
Your eyes,
My eyes,
They are a crazy color, darling . . .

Your eyes,
My eyes,
That burn

LOVE LINE

With the flame of love,
They are the color of flare,
They are fiery,
And maybe
They have burnt out the color,
They have no color, my dear . . .

They are the color of light,
They are the color of the dark,
They are the color of love,
They are passionate,
They are colorful,
They are weird color,
They are sizzling, my dear . . .

In this blazing hold of the heart
Who knows
What color are they?
Your eyes,
My eyes,
Beloved.

Probably
They are eye-color, honey.

Between Sunrise And Sunset

Bright memories of the dawn of love,
Lamps that dispel the darkness of sunset,
Meteors,
That illuminate the long road,
Shining like sparks of hope.

Let my road be smooth,
And my song sound like a proclamation,
The lights shine as hopes,
Burn like purity of love,
Be the bride of my best memories
Attractive and desirable . . .

They are attractive and glamorous,
Desirable and inspiring . . .

Whenever in the gloom of the mood
I look for hope
They chime to my ears
Like the church bells of my birthplace,
They resound
Holy, holy, singing . . .

The darkness of my mood cracks,
The meteors of my mind flashing
Like the days of my teens,
Sweet and pleasant,
Carelessly wasted
Sweet and delightful . . .

The glow of old memories,
Let them stay as they were,
Let them be careless, to remain sweet,
Like the honey taste of my first kiss.

LOVE LINE

I kissed and tasted her,
She was the girl in my mind,
She is the lass in my arms.

Warm Country

I remember with warm feelings,
That we used to play "warm country."

Barely grown out of childhood,
In our early years of schooling,
On cloudy and chilly days,
Often
We used to play "warm country."

Loud and melodized we used to repeat:
"Warm country, warm country."
Running and rushing in a group
Into the intersection of two walls of the yard,
The corner,
Squeezing each other,
Saying and repeating,
"Warm country, warm country."
Still pushing and pressing each other
Into the corner,
Warming up.

We were playing "warm country."
We were boys,
Some of us and some of the girls,
Liked to squeeze each other,
And we kept on squeezing,
We felt so good,
Saying, shouting, and repeating
With enthusiasm:
"Warm country, warm country."

With our favorite girls
The more we squeezed each other,
We desired so much more.
Clicking and pressing . . .
We could not finish the game . . .

LOVE LINE

We felt so desirable,
We were warming up,
We could not finish the game.

We were playing
Warm country . . .

From Shor To Shore

We are scattered and wandering from shore to shore,
We do not find what we are looking for from shore to shore . . .

What are we looking for, we do not know what,
We do not find what we do not know from shore to shore . . .

Where were we born, where do we live, where will we end up?
We do not know where else we will rest from shore to shore . . .

Scattered like stars, scatters in the four corners of horizon,
Where are we looking for hope and land from shore to shore?

THE SECRET OF GLITTER

You are pretty and beautiful . . . or you are not.
I do not know . . . and I do not care which one you are not.
But on your face, in your eyes, on your lips
There is a smile that captivates my soul.

It is a sparkle, it is a smile, it is a wink,
It has nothing to do with pretties or beauty.
A spark of magic that enchants,
Connecting wholeheartedly to my feelings.

And the days, and the sidewalks, the beaches
Attract with gorgeous beauty and dignity.
There are the pretties and the beauties and charms,
But the splendor remains in your grace.

The same glare persists in your looks,
Related to secrets, words, and whispers,
The days, the sidewalks, and the beaches
Keep them all close, properly flawless . . .

But you do not seem to believe to what I say, indeed,
And my whisper breaks down in a deep silence . . .
While the same shimmer again lightly
Flashes your looks with love.

Yet the tale of pretties and beauty
Is not just a fable . . . I bite my finger in uncertainty . . .
Do you know . . . do I not know . . . how else . . . ?
And I find the secret of the glitter . . .

Purple Evening

The sunset horizon is clear purple,
The mountains are purple and lustrous as ruby.

When I look at the twilight and look into your eyes,
I turn to those days full of purple and vain dreams . . .

To those days that were purple and elegant,
With longing for my remote and holy loves . . .

They were full of warmth, youth, and simplicity,
Filled with what I call with regret with madness . . .

With a madness that erupted from sacred devotion,
Love and anger were created by distilled and refined gold.

Those emotions, deepest feelings, which touch my heart,
That link up with the world and resound again.

They resound and ring with dear and good memories,
In the far horizon purple and cloudless . . .

OF HEART AND OF LOVE

I am talking
With good welfare capabilities,
That connect the present with the future
As the arch of the rainbow.

The good news is resounding
And my desires are heating up,
As the furnace of my heart and my love . . .
My bosom,
My heart and love . . .

I know the stars in the sky
Burst out
From the furnace of heart and love,
Sprinkle the sky and our bosoms
With fertile feelings . . .

We are involved in the space
With the blue of the constellation,
And cuddle each other
With light and warmth . . .
With a colorful rainbow of desires,
In illuminations . . .

It is flooded with light
Present and future,
With glittering desires . . .

I hammer on the anvil of my heart,
Gush out stars,
As hot as my dreams,
Like my heart, my love,
Like you . . .

Grish Davtian

Adorn yourself with the sparks of my heart,
With the stars of my love,
To stay warm and desirable . . .
Warm and desirable . . .
With the soft warmth of your heart,
Deep and silky
Sleek and crumbliness,
In my embrace.

PEACEFULLY

The peace you bring me is like the calm sway of the fields
That takes me away from the worries of day and night,
Takes me to my soft desires,
Close to my heart,
Just what I like.
That you embrace me with pure pleasure,
Award me the honey and wine of love
With the sweet of your velvet lips.

Squeeze me in your arms
Drown my worries,
Cover my neck with your kisses,
Touch my burning temples,
And spread your bosom on my chest.

That which is ripening
Let it last long as a clink,
That prickles me with thrills
Of my youth,
And become peaceful by ebbing
With a deep breath,
With lasting exhaustion.

Bring peace to my struggling spirit,
To enjoy my victory in love,
Gain the instinct of belonging,
Cherish your satisfaction in my domain . . .

Now with heartfelt wishes
I surrender myself to your whims
With a unique desire for sacred devotion,
I hug you
And take you beyond the rainbow
Of seven colors,
The world of flamboyant love .

Grish Davtian

Breathe my breath,
To inspire you with fertility.
I will grow a lily in the core of your heart,
And will reveal the secret of your life in blue
Reconciled in peace.
In the deep horizon of innocence
I will reward you with tranquility
As you granted me serenely.

The peace you bring me is like the calm wave of the fields . . .
The calm sway of the fields . . .

LOVE LINE

ENDURING FAIRY TALE

In these warm summer days
My heart fills up
With a cool longing for early spring,
You come to me
With the pure love of youth,
As the dew on the flower petals,
Feeling, as long ago,
Which was new to me,
Which was love, or not?

Maybe it was love,
That I had just found in my life,
That I would catch your arm,
And pull to me,
Your chest against mine,
I look deep into your eyes,
As into the mirror of the pond,
Where always, always
I feel warmer,
Melting you,
And you become mine with passion,
Refined nudity, and
Pure love.

In these hot late summer days,
My early spring cool wishes
Sway lavishly.

I conquer you with earned love,
That bloom of sweat on my chest
With unwavering fervor of loyalty.

You are always mellow,
Blossoming,
And it is enough just to touch you

Grish Davtian

By the unshakable power of the holy creation,
And you bloom with colorful flowers,
Fill my spring and summer
With the glory of beauty and pleasure.

The suns never refuse me
Along the horizons,
But they reward me with your kisses
And embraces and smiles.

Hover in my heart,
Which is the largest mass of this world,
With fathomless lucid blue sky.

No rose ever withers there,
But proliferates with noble scent,
Although temporarily,
Until you put an end to it
With a new beginning.
And the beginning is always spring.

The mornings are colorful and fresh,
Hover with me
With the wings of my just finished dream
Whose shred still lingers on my eyelids,
The world of my fairy tales is blue
And there is no end to it.

In these warm, late summer days
My cool early spring wishes
Take the ship, loaded with flowers,
To the faraway of my heart's blue sea,
Where you always sail as possessor,
Oaring with the wings of love and hope,
Immersed in pure desire
Reaching to the edge of my climax,
My emotions are like fairy tales
Without any termination.

Love Line

This good tale of my best wishes,
Sweetened with spring and summer mix,
Still tastes on my tongue
With the sweetness of your kisses
And has no end.

Grish Davtian

With Primary Love

The dawn brings the day,
The clouds are moving along the horizon
Rubbing their breasts to the summits of mountains,
Getting fertilized by pure crystal tears,
And raining their blessed fruitage
Across the fields,
On the roof of my dwelling
On the trees and roses of my lush garden.

On my lips
I can still feel the taste of your lips,
That you rewarded me all night
With melting storms.
Put your palms in mine with warm aspirations,
And cool the heat of my longings
With the soft desires of your abundance.

The gleam in your eyes opens my lips
With a new smile in the spirit of hope.
You put a new accent on my lips,
Which is the melody of my heart
And your love.

Heaven knows the number of stars,
But hides with known jealousy,
Because they are less than the gleams
Of your eyes.

You know the secret of my heart,
Which is special
With ripe assay of your sweetness.

If you want
I will disclose to the world
The deep secret of your gaze is crystal
Caused by the bright glow of your eyes.

Love Line

The meaning is bright,
I will illuminate the days of my life
With sublime love,
Which is granted as a heartbeat and breath
To my captivated spirit.

The gleam in your eyes lightens my sight
In the depths of my heart
And my gaze scatters,
My mind splashes,
Gives new depth to my sensibilities.

My heart takes me up,
See that my vein does not explode.
Do so
To match with my heartbeat
That is given to me by fidelity.

See, my temples and chest are pounding
With a love poem, with a gentle melody,
That I have gathered
From the streets of our old city,
Where my memories are scattered
At intersections,
On the sidewalks,
On your doorstep
Dear to me.

From the beginning
You were reminiscent of my dreams,
Like a flower with amazing hues of colors,
That I wore on my chest
Secret from everyone.

It blooms in the depths of my heart
As an anonymous, new fragrance,
With the scent of life,

Grish Davtian

And delightful love,
Aromatic love.

Keep close to me, no need to hurry,
Today is a Sunday of love and rest
That is awarded with elegance from above.
All my dedications will bear fruit,
Do not despair.

Now fall deeper into my heart
And worship this holy fire,
That is blazing with unquenchable flames,
Without ashes.

Now sink deeper into my heart,
To feel the sweetness of honey,
The sweetness of sin.

Sway my heart with the wave of your love,
Cover the sea at high tide
And rise upon my chest
With all the abundance of your desires,
Which is an inheritance from Eve.
I am the same original Adam
With initial love,
Purely instinctive.

LOVE LINE

OF HEAVEN AND SEA

Blink your eyes,
So, I will notice
You are in my arms, rather than the heaven ...

You are so deep ...

You are in my arms like the world,
That has cared for me, sometimes,
That has hurt me, sometimes,
That has nurtured me in glory, sometimes.

You touch my secret longings
With a whimsical female love-play,
And cause me shiver and shudder,
I lose my mind by the sweet of guilt
And drunkenness,
That takes me to the blue sphere of nowhere,
Cleanses me from the sin of Adam,
Awakens in me the inventor human
Which resembles his creator
With the light of love and hope,
Light and faith.

Let me reconcile with you,
Feel love under your tenderness,
Ramming me into climax,
Into your arms,
Into the deep sea.

I feel suspended
Between the azure of the earth and the sea,
I am as light
As the feather in the air
Wavering by your breath
In the deep of horizon,

Grish Davtian

> Between the lips of the sky and the sea,
> Amongst the kisses
> And your softness
> In the incessant waves.

SOUVENIR

I love you with the sweetness of those days
When you were seeking for a meeting,
You were clinging to my side tightly
To feel the warmth of my endearment . . .

You looked like my dream . . .

When I spoke of love
You resembled a poem,
As a dream and reality
In the infinite horizon,
That you covered entirely.

You shared your fragrance and softness,
The desirability of which
I confessed in whispers . . .

You scented more
Than the roses.

Comfort did not sway me more
Than your bosom,
That swayed me
From rejection to welcome,
From rage to calm,
From longing to fullness,
From warmth to heat,
That was melting,
It was hot,
Purified me from roughness
Refined and clean . . .

The secrets of the stars shone,
Became clearer, flashing,
Shining in the pond of your eyes
I could hardly escape drowning.

Grish Davtian

A heartfelt memory of distant horizons,
I wrap you in purple,
I submerge you with my kisses . . .

I dedicate to you with love . . .

Desire

I want to sit under the stars
And count the sparks of your eyes.

I want to pluck the petals of the flowers
And discover the colors of your eyes.

I want to perch in the garden
And breathe the roses of your eyes.

I want to stroll on the beach
And gather the pebbles of your eyes.

I want to bathe in the sun
And feel the warmth of your eyes.

... And drink the sweet taste of your lips,
I want ...

SURVIVAL

I am the vastest island
The sun never sets upon.

Mere struggle for survival
And the knowledge of it
Grant me
Such holy vastness.

It is my heritage
As a human,
With humane qualities
Which are not acquired,
But are inherent in me,
You,
Him, her.

The whole thing is
A sense of feeling,
A feel of sensation
Which exists,
Touched and tasted.

I mean to carry on

Achievement

We no longer were our shoes,
We somehow outwear them.
Fashion, style . . . you know.

We now wear out the highways,
The tires,
The airports and runways,
Even the seas,
Face and belly and all.

We have no nostrils
For the scents of flowers,
But we inhale
Through nose and mouth
All the fumes
Vomited by cars and machines,
Jets, rockets, etc.

We have come a long way
Indeed.

Master

It is a jungle out there
Of laughs and
Of tears,
Of jealousies
From old loves
Sweet and bitter
When turned to hate.

Will I ever feel
Any of them
The same way
As before?

I know
I have lost them all
Along the path
Irrevocably.

Yet will I ever?

I better neither argue
Nor solicit,
Since the time is my slave,
And I am the master
In death.

DESPONDENCY

Autumn is falling with red and blond,
Unlike my dreams,
Which are blue;
Hold me, and kiss me,
So I can feel you,
I can see you in red and blond.

The last dews of your tears are on my lips,
The taste is bitter,
My heart fears
I may lose you forever.

Remain as you are,
Do not let autumn fall upon you;
I may not survive the weight of red and blond,
I may not manage to save you.

Just hold on to my dreams,
They are changing to hope,
Hold on to me,
So you will not feel cold and blue,
I may, or may not survive,
Yet I may still love you.

EMBRACE

Exploded in blond,
Exploded in red,
Autumn is here this year.

The brunette of summer has winged away
With swallows,
With the memories of spring.

There is redness on your cheeks,
The hues of dawns,
The shadows of sunsets;
There is flooding of colors
In my eyes
Glimmering with your approach.

You twist your waist gracefully,
Your hips float softly;
I hold your wave in my clasp.

Warmth passes through my palms,
It is the compassion of your embrace.

Love Line

SUNDIAL

I look at you with the flare of my eyes,
My watch is sundial;
I reign on my loves with warmth.

The moon is cold like the north,
Its ticking does not echo
In the delicate depths of my heart.

Make the miracle happen,
So that I can approach you
With the primordial warmth of my instincts,
Which blossoms with flickering quiver,
And reach my mind
To make my secret devotion complete.

At the threshold of the universe
It is only a relic,
An incomprehensible tremor of deep caprice,
Pure and clear,
Which will connect you with my existence,
With the concept of love and longing.

Is it that you are not feeling?
Is it that you are not the same?
Is it that you are not looking
With the flare of your eyes?
Is your watch not sundial?

Brace yourself with obedient desire,
With the waves of your mind,
With the warmth of your breath,
So that your consummation will be filled
With pleasure,
You will become a bride
With complete contentment.

Grish Davtian

> The moon is cold like the north,
> But my warm watch of the sundial is counting
> The hours
> In seconds.

INTOXICATION

It is a summer warm evening,
The stars are glittering
With the flashes of my desires.

I approach you
Like the thirsty reaching for water,
Like the traveler arriving for his rest.

I feel like falling in love,
I feel love shiver ... shiver ...

The shiver you cause me
When you kiss
My throbbing temples ...
Your lips are alluring.

Your breath warms my cheeks up.

Your voice touches the strings of my heart,
The harp of love resounds,
I tremble ...

Your softness warms me up
Like the cress of your fingers
On my spine.

I am intoxicated ... intoxicated
By the wine of your love.

Conditionally

Make me your guest someday in the dark hours
I will open the remoteness of the dim layers of your heart.

I will turn the dull dales to sunny side,
And deluge your barren wishes with light.

You have a golden glitter,
A shred of ray through the clouds
Covering me with charm,
Love, torment, and grudge.

Distant and infinite are the roads of the world,
Diverse and scattered,
With which you have not been related,
You are not in dark turbulences in an endless plunge.

You have remained on the rim of the falls,
Hopelessly suspended,
Yet with true hops.

Do not ask me to deliver your soul
If you do not want me to separate your present
From your past.

AUTUMN LEAF

Fallen from a plane tree
Autumn is a parched leaf...
She is a lovesick lass
Who has plucked out the beat of my heart.

Not a leaf, but a flower of winter,
A snow flower of untouched summits,
A falling star of diming horizons
In the icy cold of blue distances.

Not a leaf, but a flower f spring,
Blossomed in my loving heart,
Dews and drops on her petals,
Flooding my entire bosom.

Not a leaf, but a flower of summer,
Perched on a ray of the sun;
She has a romantic song
On the velvet of her lips.

Yet it is a leaf of a plane,
Adorned with the gold of puberty,
Full of autumn tears
Dropping inconsolably.

With words and letters of love
She is a promise of delight,
A holy alter of feelings,
A rainbow of luminous wishes.

Yet, she is not.
It is only a murmur
That dissipates like a dream.
A red scarf round her waist;
Is she a girl... is it a wet leaf?

Grish Davtian

> She falls on my arms,
> It flies with the wings of wind,
> It is a leaf of plane,
> She is a loving lass.

HOT WITH LOVE

I desire the flavor of your lips,
And the silkiness of your thighs,
The secret cravings of your whisper,
And the turmoil in your sight.

So that you will faint into my bosom,
In the loop of my arms,
O! it is the loop of your love
That is strangling this lover.

Your bosom, the garden of my dreams,
Is ripe with softness,
With witness and tremor
It lurs me to sinfulness.

In my palms is your bust
To bend and collapse on your chest,
To mix the thirst of my desires
With your secret yearnings too.

To feel your breathless panting,
The beat of your wild heart,
To rinse the taste of your lips,
And cool the hotness of my thirst.

LOVEFLOODED

You come and roll over me
Like the sun,
Warm and reachable like a ripe apple;
You blandish me ardently;
You do not even let me
Catch my breath.

You rinse the bunch of my lips
With avaricious desire.

I get enveloped in your warmth,
And submerge into your arms,
Flood your heart and soul,
Crumple your bosom
For survival and satisfaction.

You are not a world of dreams,
But you are the sea of life
Floating me in time,
In life.

ON THE PAVEMENTS

Wallowed on the footpaths
There are numerous memories,
Like the leaves of autumn
Scattered on the pavements.

The night and the shadows fall,
Cover the paths,
Cover the old memories
On the trails.

Unreachable

It is a misery for me
That you sit so close to me,
Yet I cannot reach you.

In that short distance
There are so many obstacles and falls
That you cannot reach me.

There are so many lines and shadows,
Memories and bygones
Accumulated between us,
That we cannot reach each other.

THE SWEET OF LIFE

Our eyes meet each other,
Our looks get nailed together,
You approach with aroma and warmth,
Like a ripe summer evening . . .
Summer evening.

Your tears fall
When I hold your elbow,
Tears of happiness . . .
Your tears.

The blue lake of my love
Is before your sight,
On the clear mirror of the water
Your tears of longing drop
And sculpture such plates
Full of the sweet of life.

Look me in my eyes,
The current of my love flows,
Fills the distance of separation,
Floods with devotion and passion
And reaches your lips . . .
Your lips.

Kiss me with chaste desire,
With blessed sacrifice of affection
To proliferate the life with future . . .
Life and future.

On the blue lake of future
The rain sculptures such plates,
Circular plates,
Full of sweet of life . . .
Full of sweet of expectancy.

GRISH DAVTIAN

> Test it with savory belief,
> As enjoyment and happiness . . .
> Happiness of being.

LOVE LINE

AMERICA THE THIRD WAY

I do not know
Whether it is a coordination
Of hope and fear
That reaches for a summit.

The point
That we do not know
Where the summit is,
Is not defined
Or
Is not designed for such purposes.

It is somewhere
That we will finally find out.

I am leading the line
For that search.

Summit, peak, top can be
Next to us.

LOVE

The far is beyond my chest,
Where I keep my most valuable,
Which is known to everybody.

I am keeping you secret,
In my chest;
Nobody knows you,
But everybody knows
Love.

You are close to me
From within,
Where the heart is
And the blood
And the feeling . . .

Love Line

WITH DIFFERENCE

It is a light shower of rain,
Which is knocking at my window,
With a reminder of a perplex intention...
Perplex intention...

Enter and you will arrive at my presence,
Which is sweet with the test of my longing...
Sweet and tasty...

After all those falls
You reached my aim
Only with that shower;
You made my aim as your own,
By which I am enriched...
Enriched...

Do not change yourself,
Do not resemble me,
Your resemblance will expand
My sadness,
I shall suffer with boredom,
I shall be satisfied with fumbling,
Because when I know by heart,
I do not look at,
I only touch lightly.

The difference fills me
With awe;
I cover it with light and love,
To distinguish it;
I do not fumble when there is light,
I observe and understand it,
I accomplish it with ceremony,
With devotion and belief...
When it is bright and luminous...

WAITING

The twilight falls like tranquility
And I am stubborn
With the desire to meet you . . .
With my desire . . .

It has been so long . . .
The sweetness has reached its dept,
The bitterness is burning my throat . . .
Burning . . .

Appear in the alley,
Disturb the slumber of the shadows,
And approach my loneliness . . .
My loneliness . . . my waiting . . .

Behold, the lamps have been lit on the pavements
Like the ripeness of the bunch of grapes in autumn,
Ripe and sweet . . .

Do not fear,
Drop from the branch of ripeness . . .
Believe me that you will fall into my arms,
And in the softness
You will not feel the fall . . .

LOVE LINE

WITH FAITH

In my discoloring clay
Resound the song of fire,
Of the sun, and
Of the rain...

Resound the gloria
And I shall wake up with delight...

I wake wp with delight
And worship you
With praising canorous canticles...
I sing... I eulogize...
I sing the song of love...

The choicest treasure of happiness
Is the truth of belief...
Believing...
And I believe...

Disengage me from the longing of remotes,
Disengage me from the loneliness of gloom,
So I shall walk the path of happiness...

The hope fills up my heart,
And I fall in love with affability,
I hold my belief
With clarity...
Clear and pure...
Clear and pure...

In my shining clay
Resound the song...
Resound the gloria...
Complete it with the song of love...

THE STAR OF DREAM

That little dream,
Which warms up your heart,
Is hanging
From that twinkling star.

Do you see
That gleaming star,
That glittering star?

Look!
Extend your hand to it,
You may catch its reflection . . .

Your little dream
Is the reflection of that star . . .

Extend your hand . . .
Extend your hand . . .
And seize it . . .

Otherwise, the star will fall down
And expire on the horizon,
Far away from you . . .

You will only feel the smell of its burning . . .
Your nostrils will ache,
Your eyes will flood with tears of regret . . .

Stretch your hand
And seize
The star of your golden dream . . .
The twinkling star . . .

THE SPRINGS AND SWALLOWS

There are some springs
Which have their own swallows,
Which melodize
The year, the time,
Which is the life.

The life has its melody,
Its song,
Which rings like a bell,
Which is hang in our school
And chimes to educate us.

That chime has
A note of happiness,
Which is to the liking of my heart.

It is with the same emotions
That I illustrate bells
On New Year greeting cards . . .

They resound
The melody of happiness,
Which begins from our school
And expands,
Reaching our people and the time,
Who enter the classroom,
Which is the life . . .

The swallows chirp
And build their nests . . .

. . .It is us
Who fall in love,
And go to secret dates,
And test the flavor . . .

Grish Davtian

...It is us
Who form the family,
And melodize the concert,
With sonorous notes, with tempo and time,
Which is the life.

The life has its breeze,
Which whispers in our garden,
In the nursery of our school,
And caresses the trees and flowers
And roses,
Which are more fragrant
Than the dreams...

Trees, flowers, and roses,
Our wealth...

Those are our thoughts,
Our wishes,
Our emotions,
Our loves...

...which we enjoy in time,
Which is our life,
Melodized,
Resounding
And whispering...

It is with all those things
That I love the swallows,
That I love the spring.

THUNDERBOLT

First, he collides
With forceful desire
Of intoxicated endearment,
Which is an embrace
Conjoining the life . . .

And the flash explodes,
A total flame,
Shining thunder,
Which, on the page of the sky
Writes some lines of
A bright story of a distant love,
An intimate delight
Filled with the sacredness of arriving day . . .

He is that delight which becomes thunderbolt . . .

He utters hope,
And love and faith . . .

. . .He fills the distance with deep meaning,
Delicate existence
Of abundant pleasure . . .

Grish Davtian

A Beginning

I know I must begin
With the general impressions of my experience,
Felt and enjoyed,
Approximately with apprehended approach . . .

At the beginning
There is a light
Which colors
All the coming days . . .

There is a light
By which I see . . .

Although I do not comprehend fully,
But I do not fear either . . .

. . .I do not fear
Because the light is kind;
Really, I am not guilty
For not understanding;
And important is to begin.

WITH OPTIMISM

Today from the mirror
Looked at me a tired gray man,
With the sincere smile of my ancestors
As if accumulated from dept of centuries;
He promised me a new acquirement
With a daily decent depth,
With a graceful presence of security,
With a sweet saturation of trustworthiness.

The heartbeat of my optimism
And my firm zeal is from there,
Turning the wheel
With consistency for earning the life,
With a procession transfixed on goal,
Held out to the high
Shining with charm and charisma.

Award me, my Lord,
With worthy blessings
And with ripe goodness of success,
Fill my plans,
To relish with warm and pure enjoyment.

Tattletale

They rumor, they gossip with whisper
And say it has happened at night.

It is the slander of our street, where we live,
They say that in the dark corner opposite
I have suddenly coerced and embraced you . . .
I have kissed your sweet lips,
And squeezed
The lavish pomegranates of your breasts,
I have rubbed myself
Against your smooth thighs,
And have not heeded to your protestations . . .

They rumor and gossip continuously . . .
They do not even realize that we are
But young juveniles . . .

Yes! I have kissed you . . . for loving you ever so,
And hearing your wishful sighs too . . .
We have lusted and flirted, yes! so much the better,
We have tasted the red apple of love!
Indeed! At the dark turn of the street I stopped you
And rinsed your sugar lips . . .
That is all! Or is it that they will still gossip,
And remind us to wish more of what we had done . . .

. . . But at that hour! . . . what son of a bitch looked
And saw and started this whole tattletale?

BOYHOOD

In the shadow of a rock on the mountains,
In the far distances of the fields,
With bright and pure loves,
Where are you, my boyhood?

Totally lost in the play in the street,
Flies from home and the courtyard,
Burning from the maddening intrigues
Of a mischievous neighbor lassie...

He loves the word and the pen,
He is an enchanted boyish poet,
More or less with a smile on his lips,
With a spark and flare in his eyes.

A wide clearing in the forest,
A shady corner in a vale,
Close and sincere to my heart are
My boyhood blue memories...

Grish Davtian

With The Same Devotion

To Alenush

You are proceeding with the same daring
With which I gave my head to the winds;
And in doing that with smart pride
I deserted loves on the wings of the winds . . .

And I deserted flaming devotions
For a more gracious devotion,
For some more noble loves,
That were blazing in my heart.

The distant future was blue an azure . . .
I was a lover of blues . . .
Although I was attentive about the time,
Yet I was ready for sacrifice . . .

You are aspiring with the same self-sacrifice
With which I gave my heart to the seas . . .
The distant blue has captivated truly,
And the supreme of your aspirations . . .

So I bless your path fatherly,
The blessing of your saintly mother be with you too . . .
Even if you hold dust in your hand
Let it turn into gold,
For you, for your love, let be good fortune forever . . .

LOVE LINE

OF HEART AND LOVE

I am conversing with you
With good possibilities of wellbeing,
Which tie together with rainbow
The present and the future,
Bridged together . . .

The good tidings ring
And my desires become passionate,
As the furnace of my heart and my love . . .

I know that the stars of the sky are
Ablaze
From the furnace of heart and love;
They scatter the sky in our bosoms
With well-wishing fruitfulness . . .

We are included in the world,
In the blue constellation
And in each other's arms
With the good light . . .

With that light deluged are
The present and the future
With novel possibilities . . .

So I am hammering on the anvil,
Pour out stars,
Which are hot like my desires,
Like my heart,
And like my love . . .

Adorn yourself with the flashes of my heart,
With the stars of my love,
To remain warm and desirable . . .

GRISH DAVTIAN

THE THIRD HANDFUL OF EARTH

The connection of human and earth,
The mutual love of consanguinity is
By the homeland,
It has the fiery breath of the creator in itself,
Who took the earth,
Breathed into it
And created human;
From then on earth became homeland,
And the earth of the homeland
Become holy . . .

It is from there on
That we carry in our palm
The earth of the homeland . . .

In late summer afternoon,
In a Red Sunday,
When I was borne,
The sun of Iran greeted me,
Put the holy earth of Iran in my palm.

When the baby cry of mine
Rang for the first time
For the information of the world,
Hayk[1] and Ahura[2] agreed
And wrote the sacred letter on my forehead:

. . . That I am an Armenian by generation
And have been born as an Armenian,
Although away from Armenia,
But holding the Armenian earth in my palm.

---

1. *Hayk = The legendary forefather of the Armenian people.*
2. *Ahura = Ahura Mazda, Zoroastrian god of ancient Iran.*

LOVE LINE

I have been born on the earth of Iran,
And have taken in my other palm
The holy earth of Iran.
My bones have been ripened
By the glimmering fire of Iranian sun,
And the glimmering fire of Armenian sun,
On the Red Sunday of a late summer afternoon.

From the earth of Armenia
On the earth of Iran;
The holy earth of Armenia in one palm
And the holy earth of Iran in my other palm.

... The years of my half-century have passed by,
More years have passed by ...
I have wandered
Through many countries
And have entered
The American homeland of immigrants,
And established my homestead
On the holy earth of America ...

... Now ... in which palm shall I take
The third handful
Of the holy earth of America ...

I take in my both palms.

With Guiltiness

Touch me,
And pat me,
Bequeath me shiver of love,
Recite for me the song the songs
To live the real life
With its sweet elements
And flavor...

The blue of the sky is unreachable,
The stars glimmer in the azure above;
In the sapphire sea of your eyes
There are flashes of melodies...

It rings... it chimes...
There is a tingling there...

I hear,
But I cannot find...

In the dome of my soul,
In somewhere,
The bells are ringling
With the clapper of love...

Your desire, like the chimes of love,
Recites hymns
And blend with my songs,
With my wanting and quest...

You are that sin
That knowingly
I commit unwillingly...
Wishing...

Love Line

If loving is sin
You are the sin;
Otherwise I only pray,
I love . . .

That you touch me,
And pat me,
Bequeath me shuddering quiver,
An unending, close shiver and play . . .

You are the flavor of the deepening and life,
I drink it with enjoyment;
You are the salt of my wishes,
The taste of devotion
And the sin of desire . . .

I seek and find,
I possess
The mad and licentious trick of life . . .

You touch and caress
With the warmth of consolation,
The warm consolation . . .

SENTIENCE

You swing in my memory
Like a feather
Light, soft and evasive . . .

From the slightest inflection of my breath
You fly to hopelessness,
In the space and in my mind,
With the most vibrant volume of memories.

For example, I remember, that
We were gathered together,
We were looking at each other,
It is more a usual thing,
Friendly, intimate, and calculating . . .

But when I was looking at you,
Everybody was noticing
That I was looking at you . . .

Yet, when I was not looking at you,
Everybody was feeling
That I was wishing to look at you . . .
It was so much felt . . .

The current of my stare,
The tide of my desires
From my heart towards you,
Towards your face, eyes, and lips,
Bosom, thighs . . .
. . . Eyes . . . lips . . .
Was felt
In the atmosphere . . .
That I wished to look at you
Was so much felt,
It was so much noticeable
That I was looking at you . . .

LOVE LINE

My desires were felt
In the atmosphere and in my heart,
Within the spaces between us all;
My desires were seen
In the shimmers of my stares,
Which were glimmering . . .

I was feeling that your eyes were sparkling . . .

We all were talking together,
We all were looking at each other,
Which is more a usual thing;
And it was a usual thing
If we were to get up and go,
Or if one of us were to get up and go . . .

When you got up and went
It was felt in the atmosphere
That, there, I would also get up
And go after your footprints . . .

And it was felt
That that was why
You got up and went,
Taking my gaze with you . . .
As everybody eye witnessed . . .

Nobody made any remark . . .
We all were feeling,
The current was in the atmosphere
And in my heart . . .

And . . . just like a usual thing,
As everybody felt and expected,
I, too, got up and went after you . . .

Red Apple

The red apple of love,
Of your lips, is ripe,
Emblazoned with the fire
Of my wants and wishes . . .

Softly touched
The doves on your chest
Nestles next to my heart
Feeling its warming beating . . .

I am breathless of passion . . .

In front of my embrace
Open yourself up
To the edges of your love
So I may reach you . . .

The waves are carrying me,
Carrying me to the depths,
Swaying me up and down . . .

The coast is undulating,
Fluctuating,
Fluctuating passions and extents . . .

Stretch out your hand
So I may hold it,
Lest I get swallowed by the sea,
So I may at least reach your coast
To embrace your slim waist
To bite with hunger
The red apple of love . . .

I am floating in the sweetness,
The distance is coming close to me,

Love Line

The stars are clambering
In my eyes . . . in your eyes . . .
Suddenly the ray fractures
And the mist covers . . .

I recover my consciousness,
I wake from slumber,
Longing for tranquility
Which breaths with your scent,
And gives me your flavor . . .

On my tongue I feel the flavor of
The red apple of love . . .

GRISH DAVTIAN

OF SKY AND SEA

Blink your eyes
So I may notice
It is you in my arms instead of the sky...

You are deep indeed...

You are in my arms like the world,
Which sometimes cherishes me with love,
Which sometimes causes me pain,
Which sometimes covers me with glory...

You touch my secret longing
With womanly capricious love play,
And cause me hair-raise and thrill;
You take my senses away
With sweetness of sin
And intoxication,
Which take me
To the unlimited blue sphere,
Refines me, cleanses me from Adam's sin,
Awakens inside me the creator-man,
Which looks like his creator,
With the bright faith of love and hope...

Let me coalesce within you,
So that your caresses will enamor me
And hurl me into climax...
Into your arms... the sea...

As if I am suspended
Between the azure of the sky and the sea...
I am light like the feather in the air
As if floating from your breath
Between the kisses of the sky and the sea...

ANXIETY

Although it is inopportune,
And the doubt knocks at my heart,
Yet with an explicit hope
I cling to your promise
That you will come . . .

So I keep my lamp lit in the window
As a beacon for the lost . . .

It will be by the light of my love
That you will finally find your way
And reach my heart.

My anxiety is pounding
With the anguish of my waiting;
I wish you to appear
And deliver me
From the swamp of hopelessness,
Which is growing out of doubts . . .

I am in a nightmare,
I am wishing to dart out into the road
Of forgetfulness and loss;
But my feet have tuned to stone,
So I remain motionless,
I remain as the rock of existence . . .

O, the sunny imagination of good wishes,
Catch up and fulfill me
By the worth of my devotion,
That I have kept pure and clean
In the duration of my life,
Like the purity of the sight of my eyes
Directed to you . . .

Grish Davtian

I am caressing you with my longings,
With the warmth of my palms,
And with the love of my heart,
Do arrive and fill the emptiness . . .

My lamp is lit in the window,
And is spreading the light of love . . .
Do find the road of my heart
And arrive
As award and prize.

LOVE LINE

CHARMED WITH SECRETS

You are in my arms with tale of distant good bygones
That we have kept secretly in the depths of our hearts . . .

In the colorful shred of it we have kept a concealed ray,
And a secret that has attracted us with the miracle of love . . .

When you promised me in whisper, as if the breeze murmured,
Charmed with the dreams of past and future . . .

What you said I remember; yet I do not want to know,
In order to rediscover it by forgetting the entire world . . .

That there was . . . there was not . . . a tail of miracles,
That I killed the dragon . . . and made you mine lovingly . . .

In the labyrinth of my loves you put flames in my heart,
Connecting the prime climax with the achievements of today . . .

You seize my rosy memories out of the sky like narcissus,
And scatter them on my chest, lips, and eyes . . .

The bright stars twinkle, the falling stars leave their trace,
Clouds and sky get mingled, and disperse dew in the mist . . .

They enthuse our lives to live with enjoyment,
With the aroma that enchants and charms with secrets . . .

Of Swan

You are beautiful
Whenever you glide
On the sea of my admiration,
With your discrete and reserved majesty,
Like the swan
With soft and stretched smoothness,
Rich with curvature
And falling spiral . . .

You drive me to seduction
With your swan-like grace . . .

My desires undulate
In the blue lake of your narration,
Where the vessel of my being swings
By your caprice of
Given and declined promises . . .

It is the breath of the breeze and the lake
That blows with tender gasp,
And caresses me charmingly . . .

It is the play of the lake and the fish,
Leaping with the wave,
Snatching the sunray
And smashing it into my sight . . .

You are beautiful
Like the swan
Whose feathers have become
The pen of my love-song and my desires;
While the willow on the lakeshore
With carelessly hung branches
Reflects your image in my view . . .

Love Line

The swan glides majestically
On the lake of my feelings,
Its delicate curly neck
Against the soft caresses of the breezes,
Whereas you bend on my shoulder
Rub your breasts against my chest,
The tenderness of your hips' crumbles
And the last word of your rejection
Breaks down . . .

. . . And your hands touching,
Disturbs the lake of my soul,
And you glide
Like the swan,
And the trembling lake of my desires
Deepens in your eyes,
While submerging in my arms . . .

Striptease

The tawny autumn is a flirting girl
Which throws away shirt and skirt
And strips.

Is it of hot?

She opens her smooth breasts,
Dainty legs,
And her marble hips,
Barely leaving a pale fig leaf
As cover.

The breeze gusts,
Heaves, rumbles bashfully,
Sinning furtively . . .

The tawny autumn in her puberty
Is a flirting girl,
And I do not know
Does she keep
Or throw away the fig leaf?

The lusting shy does not look,
Does not see.

O, my temples
Pound with hot blasts,
And pounds my heart
Breathless, frantic, and love-drowned
In the still expanding
Velvet flames of autumn.

And again
A bud bursts open,
Warms up with rosy love fervor,
The redness fades with blushes.

Love Line

Is it the midday honeyed sun?

A flight of bees chimes
In the blood,
Moans in my temples,
Coquettes,
Teases playfully . . .

The tawny autumn is a flirting girl,
It reddens and crimsons,
Shades her petals and foliage,
Strips,
But . . . bashfully leaves a fig leaf
On me.

Nightmarish

*For the millions of Armenian Martyrs of
The Armenian Genocide of 1915-1924,
Committed by Turks of the Ottoman Empire & the Republic of Turkey.
A dialog with the Turks.*

The torrential wave of blood pounds my chest,
Stirring furiously from depths of the desert of Deyr al Zohr,
Rising from the dry sand, the slashed breast of my holy mother,
Wherefrom my orphaned brother received his dreadful sustenance.

Sustenance from the slashed breast of my holy mother . . .
Raped and ravished . . .
Instead of vivifying milk of love
He suckled bitter drops of coagulated and suppurated sacred blood,
The curse of an atrocious word for the mankind.

My orphaned and wretched brother satiated with vengeance,
Who otherwise would have incensed like a censer,
His pure eyes, luminous and compassionate of old
Were filled with poison of rancor, perfidious, gloomy, and dark.

Alas, my loves of springs . . . Alas, my desires for life . . .
How should I embrace you with docile and sweet enjoyment yet again?
Whereas my brother, who is myself, has identified with my horrid revenge
Suckled from the slashed breast of my holy mother . . .

THE DANCER

Plucked her gasp from an azure dream,
The dancer is an incarnate song, alluring,
She interprets a sublime mystery
By her graceful stature of a princess.

The soft tune breaks off the clouds,
And cracks suddenly like a thunder,
Crashes indomitably, full of fire,
Which burns feelings and love.

The soft modulation slides again,
Asking for caresses and consolation,
Nestles on my chest with jealousy
And unveiled lust and consummation.

Again she takes momentum obstinately,
Sliding softly and submissively,
Captivates me with her power of charm,
And makes me a worshiper of her alter.

She turns aside with flexible course
And hangs from my neck, in my arms,
She is divine in her intoxication,
Wandering around me in tides.

She embraces my soul with a horrific dash,
In the deep whirlpool of unending rhythms,
And scatters it on her charmer skirt
Like drops of light in a delight of blue.

LOVE

I knew
That you are like fire,
That should not be touched,
That you will burn.

But my desire was much,
And my love was much.

So I touched.

Do you see
How beautifully I am burning?

INFLAMED SUMMER

The summer is torrid of my hot love,
Sizzling and scorching from my roasting passions;
The sun has fallen into the forest of my love,
And has started a ruthless fire.

I am unable to distinguish your eyes from the sun,
They are so shining with the flame of love,
It is from my love that bonfires have erupted
In the dept of your eyes, with the heat of summer.

The summer is hot of the searing of my love,
Your caressing is warm, and your bosom is warm,
My heart has blossomed to the edges of the sky,
The fire of my love is much so in the summer.

It is of the burning of my love that the summer is torrid,
Upsurging with blistering of my elements;
The sea in my bosom is flooding from the deep,
Overflowing my spirit with a torrential storm.

The summer has fallen into the fire of my love,
Become red hot of your love,
I am not feeling the hot of summer,
As the furnace of my heart has wholly erupted.

FIREWORKS OF LOVE

Let me take you in my arms
And raise you to the sky,
So you can play with the stars,
So I can light stars in your eyes
That will reflect in mine.

Let me hang the rainbow
From your delicate shoulders,
Put my hand around your waist;
Let me undo the buttons
Of your flower-patterned shirt.

Fired with wishes and yearnings
To bend over your soft chest
With the sultry and swelter of my love,
To put a bond of kiss
On your sweet and alluring lips.

To tickle you with warmth and hotness,
To make you breathless panting,
To fire your desires
With the flames of real love,
With the flames of real love.

PREVALENCE

Rainy days,
And days of sunshine,
They just blink and go by,
It is the spirit of person, which remains
Solid on the rock of personality
And character.

Look at the sky,
At the stars glittering
Like hope and inspiration,
And reach for them;
Do not morn a falling star,
Because it is not a fall,
But a flight over the rainbow of luck.

Be the flying star of hope and inspiration,
Believe in deliverance
And prevail in the straggle
Of creation and life.

Zoom toward bright horizon
To insert the meaning of happiness
In the daily boredom of repetitions.

Rainy days,
And days of sunshine,
Walk through them
Strait and tall.

Cleaned Page

There are some pasts, that
Do not return
Even in memories.

Maybe you are one of those.

Like a black spot.

I am content in my hearth,
That like a black spot
You do not appear
On the white pages of my memory.

HOPE AND GLIMMER

Do not deprive yourself of hope,
And do not deprive him of hope.
Maybe that is
Your and his only possession,
Hang from just a ray
In your and his heart.

Hope is just a ray,
That has entered into my heart.

There is no heart without a glimmer of hope.

Without such vibrant ray
People will turn dark;
And although the universe will not darkle,
But will lose a ray.

The fear of obliteration
Germinates from hopelessness,
Begets hate and anger,
Sterile and destructive.

Indulge yourself in a day of peace,
Do not make your supreme decisions
In the nightmare of
Hopelessness,
Lightlessness.

Here hope will twinkle,
The little star of your fortune will flicker,
And in the light of peace
You will formulate your wishes
And your devotion.

Grish Davtian

The blue bird will hover
And flutter in the dimension of your heart,
And the sun,
It will peck iridescent rays,
It will perch on a beam of light,
Which is reflected from future.

With a trendy intuition
Rise and view yourself,
Notice the buds
Blooming as roses
In a complete flourishing,
Correlating colorfully with your heart,
Your hope and your light,
That might be your and his only possession.

ROSES PERFUME

The breeze of my feelings
Touches me,
Perfumes.

The wave of my wishes
Collides with me,
Perfumes.

Was that not that they used to
Wash the feet of the arriving traveler
And anoint his head with oil;
That washed and anointed Jesus
To relax and rest,
And perfume.

Tranquility perfumes with peace,
Which is the merit of blessed life,
Sparkling in the eyes of children.

At the end of a good day
The sunset is varnished
With colors.

The brimless purple descends
As a royal pleasure,
And erases
The dividing line of the heaven and earth,
Covers the horizon with impossible bliss of wishes,
Which is the infinite flowerbed of life.
It perfumes.

The roses of aromatic garden of life
Perfume.

GRISH DAVTIAN

> Approach me with caress
> And endow me your sweetness
> To fill my gratification with your perfume.

... In Order To Kiss

The shadows of my sadness have crowded up
Like the slow-moving bevies of autumn;
The falling leaves swamp my heart
With dry bitterness.

I am grieved like a sacrificial lamb
That is being fed with the last pinch of salt.

The thirst is pain on my lips,
The frequency of mirages
Darken my vision.
Regrets of the past accumulate
With anxiety and alarm ...

Where are you,
Termination of my quests,
Adorn my forehead with colorful decorations,
Caress my torments
With softness of your endearments,
Approach me, approach me,
And present your lips
To my kiss of satisfaction.

The Singing Angel

The beautiful angel is singing
With the other two,
The song of
Life and happiness,
Joy and pleasure.

She is beautiful
With the gleam of her eyes,
With the sweet of her kissable lips,
Scenting with the red of
Rose petals.

Bright as the colors of rainbow
Adorned with fortune
Life is emanating from
The heart of the beautiful angel
As balm and manna.

Stars are sparkling
In the ponds of her eyes;
Her lips are opening
Like rose buds.

The beautiful angel is singing.

Love Line

THE AMERICAN PULSE

It pounds from oceans to oceans,
From seas to the straits,
To the great lakes,
To the gulfs.

It pounds with the rhythm
Of my heartbeat and love,
Under the star-spangled blue
And the sky,
In the stripes
Of red and white,
Blood and peace,
As sacrifice and worthiness,
With devotion, dedication
And recognition.

My heart hovers
On the wings of bald eagle,
From oceans to oceans,
From seas to the straits,
To the great lakes,
Across the gulfs.

It pounds
Like the rhythm
Of my hearth and love.

Grish Davtian

✪ ✪ ✪

Your cheeks are colorful like the apple,
Your lips are juicy like the apricot,
As an arch of rainbow in the sky of love,
You are melting in my embrace like a snowflake.

www.ingramcontent.com/pod-product-compliance
Lightning Source LLC
Chambersburg PA
CBHW060519090426
42735CB00011B/2298